D0839815

Past
LIVES
with
PETS

About the Author

For two decades Shelley Kaehr, PhD, has worked with thousands of people around the world, helping them achieve greater peace and happiness in their lives.

Her past life regression process has been endorsed by Dr. Brian Weiss, who called her work "an important contribution to the field of regression therapy."

A world traveler, Shelley believes the soul longs to return to places from prior incarnations. She coined the term *Supretrovie* to describe sudden recollections of prior lives while traveling, and she believes all people, whether they consciously remember it or not, have flashbacks from prior lives while going about their daily business.

Shelley received her PhD in parapsychic science from the American Institute of Holistic Theology in 2001. She is a certified clinical hypnotherapist and trainer, and lives near Dallas, Texas. She truly believes we all have the ability to make positive changes and live the life of our dreams.

Visit Shelley online:
https://pastlifelady.com
Connect on her Facebook Fan Page: Past Life Lady
Instagram: shelleykaehr
YouTube: Past Life Lady
Twitter: @ShelleyKaehr

SHELLEY A. KAEHR, PHD

Past
LIVES
with
PETS

Discover Your Timeless Connection
to Your Beloved Companions

Llewellyn Publications
Woodbury, Minnesota

First Edition
First Printing, 2020

Book design by Samantha Penn
Cover design by Kevin R. Brown
Part page art by Llewellyn Art Department

Llewellyn Publications is a registered trademark of Llewellyn Worldwide Ltd.

Library of Congress Cataloging-in-Publication Data (Pending)
ISBN: 978-0-7387-6450-4

Llewellyn Worldwide Ltd. does not participate in, endorse, or have any authority or responsibility concerning private business transactions between our authors and the public.

All mail addressed to the author is forwarded but the publisher cannot, unless specifically instructed by the author, give out an address or phone number.

Any internet references contained in this work are current at publication time, but the publisher cannot guarantee that a specific location will continue to be maintained. Please refer to the publisher's website for links to authors' websites and other sources.

Llewellyn Publications
A Division of Llewellyn Worldwide Ltd.
2143 Wooddale Drive
Woodbury, MN 55125-2989
www.llewellyn.com

Printed in the United States of America

Other Books by Shelley A. Kaehr, PhD

Meet Your Karma: The Healing Power of Past Life Memories

Lifestream: Journey Into Past & Future Lives

Supretrovie: Externally Induced Past Life Memories

Familiar Places: Reflections on Past Lives Around the World

Reincarnation Recollections: Geographically Induced Past Life Memories

Past Lives with Gems & Stones

I dedicate this book to all the lovely creatures in the animal kingdom and the people who love them. I hope we can continue to learn more about the incredible species on our planet and be constantly reminded of how blessed we are to be able to share our earth with Mother Nature.

CONTENTS

EXERCISE LIST

CHAPTER FIVE

CHAPTER SIX

ACKNOWLEDGMENTS

This book came about thanks to the visionary leadership of my dear friend and editor Angela Wix. Thank you! To Bill Krause, Terry Lohmann, Annie Burdick, Lynne Menturweck, Kat Sanborn, Jake-Ryan Kent, Sammy Penn, Sami Sherratt, and the incredible team at Llewellyn, there are no words to express my gratitude. As always, I am indebted to my family and animal-loving friends, including Jim Merideth, Pat Moon, and Paula Wagner.

Introduction

OUR PAST LIFE
CONNECTIONS TO ANIMALS

PAST LIVES WITH PETS began with a conversation with friends when I explained how much I would love to come back in a future lifetime as my cat, BisKit. After overcoming humble beginnings at the local animal shelter, he quickly evolved into one of my great loves and now enjoys a life anyone would envy. I wait on him hand and foot, carry him around while constantly fussing over his food, making sure every little thing is exactly as *His Majesty* prefers. And heaven forbid I should stop brushing him before he's ready. In the case of that unfortunate event, he swipes at me until I resume my duties, and continues to do so until he deems my work complete and acceptable to his incredibly high standards. And heaven forbid I should ever dare walk by him with food he wants. He psychically tunes in and bursts straight out of his feline coma to swat my legs until I share.

In addition to his demanding nature, BisKit has several unusual behaviors, including a distinctive taste in music. He loves Vedic chanting from India and paradoxically avoids fish and tuna like the plague, insisting on a diet solely consisting of beef. He loves grazing on grasses and is so quiet I thought he was mute when I first got him. I eventually heard him meow in extreme distress at the sight of another cat in my yard. A man of very few words, he only speaks on occasion, making a gruff grunting that sounds more like a buffalo than a cat.

Before her death, his female predecessor, Goo, adored the Gregorian chanting music of the Benedictine Monks of Santo Domingo de Silos and spent several hours intently watching the funeral of Pope John Paul II on television, not once taking her eyes from the ceremony, not even for a catnap. BisKit runs in the other direction if I play my monk music, acting like I've personally offended him.

If you and I were to chat, I'm sure you'd tell me all sorts of weirdly bizarre but cute things your favorite pet likes and dislikes. Have you ever stopped to consider those idiosyncrasies may originate from past life behavior? Our pets are born with distinct personalities and tastes, even though such preferences could not have been influenced through what developmental human psychologists would call nature vs. nurture. Like people, animals often display strangely eccentric personalities.

For years I've been joking about the fact (or I should say *fact to me*) that my last two cats are "people" I've definitely known in previous lifetimes, because any soul who inspires me to such single-minded devotion is absolutely someone I've been around the block with a time or two before. Later in the book I'll reveal what I discovered about my past life connections to my two dear felines.

I'm sure you've noticed that people are often willing to do more for their pets than they are for their own spouses, friends, family members, or even themselves. You may feel the same way about your own animals. Why is that? It's a question I've wondered about. I had to ask myself— could a past life connection be the actual root cause of this obsessive love? I say yes, absolutely!

In my private practice, dozens of clients shared their beliefs that they, too, knew their pets before in other lifetimes. Sometimes the memories of these lives floated into their consciousness automatically, and on other occasions, they emerged as part of longer sessions while dealing with other life issues. After doing past life regression for twenty years, I assure you my clients never ever come to see me because of an issue with their pet. Let's face it. Our pets are typically the one solid source of happiness in our lives.

During regression sessions, I guide people through a process I first talked about in my 2003 book, *Lifestream: Journey Into Past & Future Lives*. Clients travel into several past lives to discover connections to other people, talents, and gifts they had in the past that could potentially be utilized in the present or find the source event of some much-needed healing. The purpose for visiting the past is not to become stuck there. The information is used to empower people to live fuller, more meaningful lives in the present.

One way this happens is when clients meet spiritual guides and helpers to gain further insight into their soul purpose. Actions from past lives can often demonstrate the client's soul purpose; then they access current life situations when they also experienced themselves living up to their potential; finally, clients progress into their current life futures to see how they are able to best continue to utilize the information received from their session for the highest good of all concerned.

The imagination is the only limit to what past life regression can achieve. The more open clients are to exploring the information received, the greater the potential for transformation. Of course, no hypnotic regression can take the place of a doctor's care or assistance for mental health issues. I see any alternative healing as a supplement to assist people in developing understanding and to learn techniques to help maintain a more peaceful state of mind since hypnosis is so akin to meditation. Pet connections typically come up as a sidebar and a happy and unexpected surprise.

Another important aspect to note is that, unlike some regressionists who spend countless hours verifying each and every detail of their cases, digging around in an attempt to prove the validity of each case according to historical record, my work is more focused on healing and transforming challenging life issues. Rather than trying to prove every little detail of the client's story, I assist them in finding greater inner peace and happiness within their souls. When clients are asked certain questions, stories emerge in their minds that include pictures, thoughts, and feelings. There is no way to know for sure where those images come from or how to differentiate a deep, embedded memory of something that actually happened versus the tapping into of some archetype that resonates with the client during their journey. I encourage my clients to be open about what they discover because everything that comes up is important to the story of their soul.

Whether a story is real or not, there is always a reason why certain images appear during the hypnotic journey. Some visualizations can be taken literally, while other concepts are more symbolic. Both hold merit. While I do pay attention to historical accuracy in the cases you'll see in *Past Lives with Pets*, please know that in some cases the client's observations are coming from aspects of their Higher Self and subconscious mind and are not literal representations of historical events.

One of the big influences on my life and my eventual decision to become a past life regressionist came after I read the book *The Search for Bridey Murphy*. The subject of that work had allergies and went to times in ancient Ireland to find relief. She recounted an abundance of details about the little village where she supposedly lived, and invariably, skeptics discredited her and said she was merely picking up on things she had read in books, and information she had obtained from third-party sources. From my perspective, the biggest value of her experience came in the fact that she no longer suffered from her allergies after her transformative regression. Likewise, my private practice goal is to help clients find peace through these processes, and I know from years of experience that regression absolutely works.

After collecting random case histories about animals over the course of many years, once I began to seriously entertain the idea of writing this book, I created a survey to find out more about the connections to animals and the belief that people know their pets from past lives. My survey posed three questions:

1. Do you believe animals have souls?

2. Do you believe you've known your pets in a prior lifetime?

3. Do you believe your current pet is a reincarnation from a pet you had earlier in your current lifetime?

Not surprising, 100 percent of the respondents believed animals have souls. Eighty percent believed that they had indeed lived previous lifetimes with their current life pets, and 25 percent believed that they've had the same soul show up in two different pets during their current lifetime. Several clients explained that their current dog or cat is without a doubt the same exact soul of a pet they lost years prior.

In a follow-up survey, I asked the following:

1. Do you believe it's possible to have lived in non-human form in a past incarnation?

2. Do you believe you've been an animal in a past life?

Two-thirds of respondents believed it's possible to have lived in a non-human form in a prior lifetime, while only a third believed they were animals in past lives.

These questions, along with the case histories I've collected through the years, formed the material for *Past Lives with Pets*. In all my books, the client names and unique personal details have been changed to protect their identities.

During our time together, I hope we will have some fun exploring our collective pet fixation. I break the pet phenomenon down by analyzing several key areas:

1. People who gazed into their pet's eyes and knew they had known their dog, cat, horse, etc., in a past life and decided to have a past life regression to uncover more details, or clients

who'd discovered by accident the huge role a pet played in their soul journey during a past incarnation.

2. People whose current life pet passed away, and sometime later, the same soul showed up in a new body as the reincarnated version of their earlier pet.

3. Past life case studies where other kinds of animals played an important role in the client's soul journey that profoundly affected their current life conditions.

4. Clients who experienced themselves as animals in prior incarnations.

5. Animal Spirit Guides who appeared to clients with messages of hope and encouragement.

6. Grief healing for those who had suffered the loss of a pet.

For the many years I've worked as a past life therapist, I've run across several cases of these fascinating phenomena.

Although this book is filled with case histories of pets, I assure you, people never ever seek a past life regression solely and specifically to uncover the source of their relationship with their pet. The stories you will read about in this book are excerpts of longer regression sessions where my clients delved into the vastness of their souls to arrive at the source of various issues and, because our pets love us unconditionally and often provide us with some of our best relationships, people only discover these connections when they're part of a larger issue.

Human nature is such that we typically won't work on ourselves unless we're trying to move out of pain. Pets often provide us with tremendous joy in our lives, which, sadly, is sorely missing from much of daily experience. This book celebrates that love and urges you to appreciate and cherish the lessons our lovely animals give us by teaching us how to be more open and loving in the world at large.

During these sessions, clients are pleasantly surprised when they happen upon a pet they've known before or are able to reconnect with a pet that crossed over. Most of the animal lovers I know truly believe without a doubt their pet is a kindred spirit housed in animal form, and those beliefs are strengthened after visiting past life events.

Even in our current lives, the presence of our animal companion provides stabilizing support during our darkest days; it's a soul who is truly beside you during the best of times and the worst of times. Interactions with other people can be quite challenging because each soul brings their own past experiences and karma into the relationship. Animals are pure love and allow us to put our whole selves into loving them, and they in turn reflect those affections back to us in a way that often feels more satisfying than our human connections.

Overall the dealings we have with animals are universally designed to help us become better people and stewards of our planet, the environment, and each other.

Belief and Areas of Exploration

Once I discovered that so many people believed they'd known their pets before and had perhaps been animals themselves in prior lifetimes, I was curious to study cultural beliefs to see how prevalent such beliefs are in various world religions. Not surprising, the Eastern religions that support the belief in reincarnation also cited the idea of a soul's journey, including life in animal form.

The Hindu religion definitely acknowledges the idea that a soul can begin in animal form and can evolve into a human being based on doing progressively good works such as being kind to others and avoiding harming any living beings. The belief in good works is common to all religions, yet Hindus also believe that lying or treating others badly could cause the soul to devolve into an animal form in a future incarnation. Children are warned if they don't behave they will receive a bad future lifetime as punishment for misdeeds.

Buddhists share similar beliefs to the Hindus and others about why animals are lesser forms of consciousness by acknowledging that all beings suffer from either craving certain outcomes or having aversions to things. What does that mean? People get attached to outcomes and when things fail to manifest, they feel miserable. Likewise, when we run away from things that are offensive to us, we create a different kind of misery.

The difference in human and animal consciousness is obvious for Buddhists. The human being has the power to reason through the cravings and aversions and arrive at the middle path, where they feel neutral toward anything that happens by controlling emotions, both good and bad, and training the mind to bend to the will. By doing so, enlightenment is achieved. When Buddhists say animals are a lower life-form, that's not to say they're not wonderful creatures but they do not possess the mental ability to change their cravings for food, sex, or the killing instinct, nor can they avoid aversions by reasoning their way through unpleasant sensations.

Buddhists also believe that by doing good works and maintaining a place on the Middle Path where they do not judge things one way or another and maintain a calm state of neutrality, they eventually transcend the need to incarnate and arrive in the heavenly state of nirvana, where they are free of suffering and experience ultimate peace, tranquility, and happiness. Animals cannot do this because they cannot control those urges. Therefore, the only way to achieve nirvana and enlightenment and karmically rise above the challenges of life to arrive at a place where you are free of the constant cycling of death and rebirth is by transcending cravings and aversions by experiencing life in human form and working on self.

Followers of Jainism share similar beliefs to Buddhists and many Hindus. They follow vegetarianism and share the belief that humans have all capabilities of reasoning and senses and are therefore held to a higher standard in regard to treatment of other beings on the planet.

Transmigration is the term used in the Taoist religion to describe the belief that matter never dies, it merely changes form; therefore, you and I can indeed become animals in other incarnations. There are three worlds—desire, form, and formlessness—and the Animal Way is one of many options available within these worlds.

Another area explored later in the book is the idea of Animal Spirit Guides and watching for signs from the animal kingdom. Humans found ways to find meaning in the natural world and often assigned godlike qualities to various animals.

Those beliefs are more shamanic in nature and are shared by people throughout the world. I spent much of my early career studying the Polynesian religious beliefs in Hawaii, and in those cultures the ancestors were seen as animals in nature and were worshiped. In Japan's Shinto religion, rather than reincarnation, they believe in Kami, the spiritual energy in all things that recycles after death. They worship a wide pantheon of Spirit Animals. Even the Hindu religion cites certain animals as being gods.

Grief Recovery and Loving Our Pets

One of the major focuses of *Past Life with Pets,* other than the obvious, *pets,* deals with grief, which is one of the main reasons I became a past life regressionist in the first place. When I was in my mid-twenties, a friend of mine passed away. At that time, I had very little experience with death or loss other than what I had experienced through my pets. I couldn't handle my emotions very well. I can't even begin to imagine how traumatic that death would have been had I not already lost my fish, cats, dogs, rabbit, gerbil, and other pets over the years, because up to that point, I hadn't experienced the loss of any other close friends or family members. I'd never even been to a funeral. Some may call that lucky, and in a way, that's true, but being in my mid-twenties with no point of reference for what to do with so much grief made the feelings overwhelming and impossible to handle.

After searching and struggling for years, past life regression gave me a tangible point of reference to help me understand why things happen as they do. I adopted a belief that things happen for a reason, even when that reason defies logic. My regression provided a deeply personal experience of the fact that we all have a time to live and a time to die, and that all major life events will happen to everyone and all in divine order.

Over the years, I've had some wonderful pets—several cats, a few dogs, lots of fish, a gerbil, and a rabbit. Each one proved special in his or her own way, and one thing they all have in common, regardless of breed and type, is that they all left way too soon. With such short life spans, the family fish, in particular, taught us that a big part of life is about saying goodbye. That's one of the hardest aspects of owning any pet. By nature, our loving animals do not share the same lengthy lifespan we do (unless of course you own a parrot or a certain type of turtle) and therefore, animals become some of our greatest teachers to help us learn how to deal with and hopefully recover from grief and loss. Pets become members of the family, so it's no wonder people suffer so much when they pass.

Death isn't the only kind of loss our pets help us survive. During my teens and twenties, I had a cat my family nicknamed the Scruffster. The Scruffster helped me get through the death of my friend and lived until shortly after my divorce. She played a huge role in my life and picked her exit just as I had finished a major turning point in my journey.

Years ago, someone told me that all relationships will come to an end at some point, either through death, divorce, or by people simply drifting away from each other. The sentiment was meant to encourage me as I navigated the choppy waters of my own divorce. Over the years when counseling clients, I've found myself reminding them of this important fact any time they're dealing with grief. Loss of anything we've grown accustomed to can be hard to handle, but we can find some solace in understanding that nothing lasts forever, and change is the only constant in this world.

Once the Scruffster went on to greener pastures, my next major relationship happened when my cat Goo came into my life, just in time to see me through one of the most difficult chapters of my life—stage-four endometriosis. Shortly after Goo arrived, I began having profound and chronic pain that went undiagnosed for quite some time. I eventually spent over a year in and out of hospitals, either having surgery or recovering, all the while with my little fuzzball Goo steadfast by my side. Back in the day, endometriosis was not discussed and was very misunderstood. Suffice to say here, it is a horrifically painful and debilitating condition that has no external indicators and is quite difficult to diagnose.

These days, people have support groups and lots of literature to help, but back then, the struggle was solitary and painful on a physical and emotional level. Time does heal all things, but at times, there are still moments when something causes a memory to pop up from these darker days and normally I'm left with an immense feeling of gratitude for all my friends and family who stood by my side—and especially for my pet. After my final surgery, Goo was there for me twenty-four/seven. I'm sure you know what I mean. When you're going through tough times of any kind, your animal is your constant companion and support system.

We all face hardships during our lifetimes. I assume if you're reading this, you love your pets as much as I love mine, and you know that your relationships with your animals mean more to you than just about any other. It may be that nobody else is there with you during the dark and lonely nights or listens to you and really seems to understand you at a soul level in the way pets do. And when you look back on those pets you've loved who have passed on and think about all the tough times they helped you get through, well, it's enough to cause anybody to break into tears of profound gratitude and awe at how such a love can come into our lives if we're open.

Because of the depth of my unconditional love for Goo, one of my toughest losses happened several years after I'd made a full recovery. Goo saw me through my illness, through my schooling to receive my PhD, and the beginning of my career as a writer and healer. She helped me come full circle, and after all that time, when she finally passed away after a long and lingering chronic condition, I couldn't handle the loss any better than I had handled losing my friend years earlier.

At the time, I lived alone and Goo was my sole companion during a period of several years when I worked out of my house. I never ever felt alone when she was around, but once she passed, I woke up to the fact that in the real world, I lived alone, and had done so for many years with very little human contact. Who needed a human when you have your cat friend around? My real-life isolation led me to a full-blown dark night of the soul and I had never felt more alone.

While navigating through my grief, I wondered how in the world I could ever go through the loss of a pet again. I vowed I would never have another pet—a sentiment shared, if only momentarily, by just about every other grieving pet owner I know. Soon thereafter, I had a series of dreams and an increasing nagging feeling that I needed to go to my local animal shelter anyway. I tried telling myself that when I went to the shelter, I could put the question of pet adoption to rest once and for all, because surely I wouldn't find anyone I wanted to adopt. Of course, my attitude changed with a little time and extra healing. To me, no matter how miserable I might feel after losing a pet, I know there are always thousands of little animals out there who will not survive without kind-hearted people stepping up to the plate and adopting them.

I went to the animal shelter, and there he was—my soon-to-be cat—sitting in the cage. The moment our eyes met I knew he was definitely the reason why I'd had the dreams. He moved toward the bars and I rubbed his furry little ears. I sat there gazing into his beautiful eyes. I couldn't believe I'd found him that day. I tried talking myself into the idea that I'd go take a look but wouldn't find anyone special. Nothing could be further from the truth. He looked perfect and sweet. But despite our instant soul connection, emotionally, I wasn't ready to open my heart yet. I told myself Goo hadn't been gone that long. I succeeded in allowing my mind to prevail over my heart, and as a result, I suffered. That night and for the next three nights, I went home and cried my eyes out thinking about the sweet little kitty at the animal shelter. I tossed and turned in my sleep and could not get him out of my mind, so I went and adopted him a few days later.

While I could beat myself up over making poor BisKit wait, I believe the connection we share with our animals is every bit as important as the bonds with our families and closest friends. These connections are destined, and my agony about leaving BisKit that first day further exemplified that we were meant to be together and share whatever amount of our lives together as we are fortunate enough to experience.

———————

If you're an animal lover who ever wondered why you love your animals so much, you've come to the right place. Throughout part one of *Past Lives with Pets*, you'll hear the love stories of my clients and their pets and meet people who successfully came to terms with their loss and learned about themselves and their soul journeys in the process of owning and loving animals and overcoming their grief. I'll share several amazing examples that I hope will not only be entertaining but enlightening as well.

In part two, you will have a chance to go back to a place where you can meet with your beloved fur babies and hopefully find great peace and healing in the process. You will discover more about your unique connections to your favorite pets from your past and heal from hurts and traumas caused by losing your most beloved companions

Whether you're reading this for sheer amusement or because you, too, believe you've known your lovely little fur balls in times long gone, I hope you will find great enjoyment from this book and come to understand what I have—that our pets help our souls learn about the true meaning of love unlike any other relationship we have during our lifetimes. By embracing that affection and understanding the soul lessons received from our pet connections, we grow and develop on our life path.

Next up, we will explore fascinating case histories of clients who knew their pets in prior lifetimes. I hope their stories will provide you food for thought as you prepare to go through your own past life regressions in the final section of the book.

PART ONE

—————

CASE STUDIES

THE FOLLOWING SECTION CONTAINS fascinating case histories from clients who received great insight and healing by uncovering the past life connections they shared with their pets, and with animals in general.

Past life regressions involve several lifetime discoveries that often have multifaceted effects on the people who receive the information. The pet topic is something that is not always sought by the client but comes up quite often as a pleasant sidebar to the other details of the regression. The relationship challenges we all face during earthly life can be explained and examined in a deeper way when we explore them through past life regression. People often seek regression to discover how they've known certain people before and how they can best navigate the choppy waters of coexisting with others. All of us exhibit certain habits in our personal dealings, and when we view ourselves and how we respond in relationships through the eyes of the animals we love, we can gain tremendous insight into ourselves and our soul journeys.

I believe we all repeat patterns over the course of many lifetimes. Such is the case for many of the people in the following section. Animals often allow us to see our behaviors and rise up to a higher standard and way of being in the world that is more suited toward peace and tolerance. When animal relationships come through in past life memories, clients can use the information to make happier and more enlightened choices in the present incarnation, as you'll see in this next section.

Chapter One

PAST LIVES WITH CATS

WHILE WORKING ON *Past Lives with Pets*, I wanted to learn more about my past lives with my current cat, BisKit, so I used a recording of an exercise similar to the ones you'll get to try in part two. I regressed to a thick-wooded forest and my life as a young girl in 1832 Scotland. At the edge of the tree line, I saw a green, grassy pasture with a tiny log cabin that appeared to have come straight out of a Thomas Kinkaid painting. A rudimentary fenced-in area next to the cabin held our sheep, and there, clear as a bell, was BisKit: my special sheep friend whom my parents had assigned to my care. Our family raised about a dozen sheep for the wool to make sweaters and blankets, and I cared for my pet sheep by feeding, brushing, and combing him while I hugged his neck and tended to all his needs. In frigid winters, I moved him closer to our house and covered him in blankets to ensure he didn't become too cold. Our love lasted until I became ill and passed away very young. I saw myself in a small bedroom surrounded by family with my dear, heartbroken sheep outside.

In my current life, after returning from a recent trip, BisKit had become quite ill in my absence and he'd gotten so upset that I had left, I had a hard time nursing him back to health. He was more depressed than I'd ever seen him before, even though I was gone less than two weeks. He's always been needy like that, and in my regression, I saw that my early demise in Scotland contributes to what appears to be his clingy behavior. Nevertheless, I waited on him hand and foot until he recovered in about a week.

The epiphany that BisKit was a Scottish sheep surprised me, and it explained many of his strange habits. I never ever imagined I'd known BisKit in Scotland, yet once that came up in my regression, the visual was so lifelike and came straight up out of nowhere, I decided to do some research on the sheep. When I put "Scottish sheep" into Google search, sure enough, there was a photo of the big, white, thick-curly-haired animal. I noticed how the one pictured had a black nose and so did BisKit. I also saw some grey spots on its legs, and because he is grey and white this time around, the color shading seemed quite similar. Like many animals, BisKit loves eating grass and crunchy snacks flavored like "greens." Could that be from his sheep life? Who knows! He also has a big round body and cute stubby legs that angle out from his body in a way that is quite like the sheep he used to be. I was blown away.

The other cat I wanted to know about was Goo, my cat who loved the Catholic Church. She literally sat attentively for hours watching the funeral proceedings for Pope John Paul II back in 2005. I felt sure she and I knew each other during some past life in Rome, but when I went to have a regression, the results were different than I had imagined. I saw myself wandering around the Vatican as a devout Catholic pilgrim. Goo the cat lived in the stone crevasses in and around the walled Vatican City. I provided her with a few crumbs from my meager rations, and despite the fact that she lived outdoors, she actually fared quite well living off charity from all the generous people living in and around the Vatican. Her attraction to the Pope's funeral in modern times came from her soul recognition of the place where she had lived long ago.

Next you'll read some interesting stories from other people who also reconnected with their cats after knowing them in the past.

Keith and His Cat Weathered Storms

Keith lived in Florida, where his home was destroyed by a hurricane. Despite that, he insisted on staying to rebuild because he loved that part of the world. When he came for a regression, part of what he wanted to work on was his deep and justified fear of weather. The storms trashed his home and the surrounding town, leaving him homeless until FEMA provided him with temporary housing. He lost valuable equipment he needed for his business and by all counts, life as he'd known it was over. Still, he kept a good attitude in realizing that he was blessed to be alive:

"Don't get me wrong," Keith said. "I'm grateful to everyone who came and helped us get out of this mess. I'm lucky and the things I lost were just that—things. All of that can be replaced. My extended family is okay, I'm okay, and nobody I knew died in the storm, so really what's my problem? That's why I'm here. I have a deep fear I can't seem to shake. I know I should be able to resolve this; I've lived in this area for over twenty years and I've actually been through some storms worse than this one, but ever since this happened, I'm having nightmares that won't go away. In the dreams, I'm out on the high seas, in the middle of the ocean, dashing around in the waves. When I wake up, I'm sweating and panting like I can't breathe. I'm afraid for my life."

During the storm, he rescued a stray cat who, like him, was ripped from familiar surroundings. During Keith's regression to overcome trauma, he discovered that this feline friendship started far earlier than he'd initially thought. I had an intuitive feeling we needed to discover what storms he had experienced in the past, but before doing so, we went into his current life to ease some of his trauma from the more recent events:

SK: Surrounded by a protective light, knowing you are totally safe and secure, go to the day of the storm. Be there now and notice what's happening.

Keith: I'm in my house. The wind is whipping around. It's bad out there. I can hear the sirens going off, but it's way too late for me to do anything about that.

SK: Can you fast-forward to the worst time during the storm? Be there now and know you are safely surrounded by a protective light. Are you there now? If so, what's happening?

Keith: Yes. I'm crouched down in the closet near my front door. The wind sounds like a freight train outside. I wish I had evacuated, but I didn't take the warning seriously. I hear a scraping of metal and I know my gutters are being blown off the side of the house. I hear a rumble that sounds like an earthquake and a loud crash. I hear the whistling winds. I wait in the closet for a while. I don't remember every detail though. I thought I went to sleep, but I realize now I might have passed out for a while, or I can't remember..."

SK: That's fine. Fast-forward to your rescue, right after the storm when you come out, and be there now.

Keith: I'm unconscious, asleep or something, and I hear a loud knocking, then the sound of a guy's voice calling out. I try to speak and shout and let him know I'm there, but my voice sounds gruff. They find me, though, and one of the firefighters reaches his hand out and grabs mine, pulling me out. When I step out of the closet, things look worse than I imagined. My living room is ripped open and a tree is lying across my windowsill. My neighbor's roof is twisted off and it's out by my mailbox. We crunch through the debris and I see part of my roof on the other side of the house, caved in and collapsed near my garage. Everything's ripped to shreds. It looks like a nuclear bomb went off. When I go outside, that's when I hear my cat crying. Well, he wasn't my cat then. Poor thing. I had no idea where he came from. I'd never seen him before, but when I first hear him crying, I pull him out of a shrub. He's a mess—wet and scared half to death. I pick him up and hold him while the paramedics check me out. I call my family and make sure they're okay.

The storm didn't hit their area, so that's good. I stay with some of them while I wait for things to get better and I take the little cat with me. I tried for weeks to find his owner, posted ads, walked the neighborhood and everything, but nobody showed up, and we've been together ever since. That's when I named him Lucky. He's been my good luck charm and he's by far the best thing to come from that sad situation.

SK: Imagine you can lift yourself up, up, up, out of that body, out of that situation, and float over the living room. Look at your house below and imagine your angel is sending a beautiful healing light down over all your belongings, your home, everything. Allow that light to fill you up. What lessons did you learn from this event?

Keith: Gratitude. Be grateful for what you have, always. Nothing lasts forever. Stuff is not important. I should have left and evacuated when I was told to, but I was too attached to my stuff. I didn't want to lose anything. As it turns out, I lost everything anyway and I almost lost the only thing that really matters—my life. I can see now though that if I'd have left, I wouldn't have Lucky. He would've died and I think he and I were meant to meet.

SK: Is this the source event of your anxiety about storms then?

Keith: No.

SK: Very good. Imagine you can float back in time to the source of your anxiety about storms. Be there now and notice where you are, what year it is, and what's happening.

Keith: I want to say China. No, it's close to China. It's an island.

SK: What year is this?

Keith: Wow, it's really early. I am not aware because it's out of my realm of thinking at that time.

SK: BC or AD?

Keith: BC.

SK: If you had to guess, where would you say this was in relation to our modern times?

Keith: Taiwan, maybe? Somewhere around that area.

SK: Describe your life.

Keith: Simple, a fishing village. This is weird, but I see Lucky there too. He wanders around the village where I live. I feed him and he keeps me company.

SK: That's nice. Do you have a family?

Keith: Nope. Just me and the cat. Kinda like it is now.

SK: Tell me what's happening on this island at that very early time and how this relates to your fear of storms.

Keith: Living on an island in the middle of nowhere, like, that's beautiful but frightening. There's always a storm to worry about and I see myself in the village watching while a storm at sea makes its way toward us. There's nothing we can do. High winds, rain, the ocean swells. A wall of water comes and wipes us all out. We are gone, wiped off the map.

SK: Still surrounded in protective light, go ahead and float into that peaceful space in between lives. Allow your angel to send a healing light to all beings in that very early time and know that this light is washing away all fear and anxiety. What lessons did you learn on this island and how is this life affecting you now?

Keith: This is one reason why I love to live at the beach; but on some level, I remember living through that tsunami, and that's where that feeling of dread comes from. The good news, if there is any, is that I didn't have too much time to think about it back then, everything was over so quickly. In a flash we were gone, whereas in the here and now, all I do is think.

SK: How did this event relate to the nightmares you've been having? Or are they related?

Keith: Oh yes. I can see now that vision of me in the ocean water is exactly what happened. I did have some consciousness after the waves crashed over me, although not for long. My life ended pretty quickly, although it was traumatic.

SK: Are you able and would you be willing to release this energy of fear?

Keith: Yes and no. I need to respect the ocean. If I'm warned to go, then I need to listen to the authorities. I can't live in fear of every little thing, but my reason for leaving needs to change next time. I have to lose the attachment to my stuff and go because I value my life, otherwise I haven't learned a thing.

SK: Have you learned then?

Keith: I think so, yes. So long as I live near the beach, I will have more chances to be tested and I believe I'll do better in the future.

SK: Would it be okay for you to stop having the nightmares about the ocean?

Keith: Yes. I had them so I would learn, but I've learned now so they aren't needed anymore.

SK: What about Lucky? What lessons are the two of you learning about over these lives you've shared?

Keith: Friendship, unconditional love, loyalty. Having someone's back and knowing they have yours. Also, when everyone else dies and passes on, Lucky shows me that life goes on and that there's always new people and souls to meet and connect with. We're never alone and we need each other. We should help when and where we can.

SK: Nice job. Go out to your future to a moment when you have successfully achieved the balance between living with some fear and respecting nature, while still enjoying your life. What year is this and what's happening?

Keith: Next year. We're having another hurricane near here.

SK: What do you do?

Keith: I get out this time and I'm glad I do. I pack a small bag and put the cat in the car, and we head north and stay with friends.

SK: How do you feel as this is happening?

Keith: Okay. I don't care if I lose everything anymore. I don't have much anyhow these days that I can't live without, other than my cat.

SK: How is your fear level in the future when you experience rain?

Keith: I'm enjoying things more. I haven't had the problem with the rain like I did before.

SK: What happens when you return after that storm?

Keith: When we come home, everything is fine. Ever since the other hurricane, I expected the worst, but when I come back, I see some trees down and debris, but the few things I have are still intact. The great feeling is that I don't care about any of that anymore. Lucky and I go forward and it's all okay. Life's good and I'm happy to be alive.

Keith's regression helped him find transformational healing surrounding a deep and completely justifiable fear. Finding the companionship of his pet cat helped him heal from that pain and learn more experientially how important our relationships are to us during our lives. Their relationship continued to bring Keith blessings throughout the ages with the two of them bringing support and comfort to each other in times of need. This is one of the greatest gifts our animals bring us. Keith discovered what mattered most in life and the depth that love and friendship can extend to all people and beings if we open our hearts and minds.

Grieving Leslie Knew Her Cat Before

Clients often book sessions weeks in advance, but life happens between the time of booking and coming in to see me. Unfortunately, Leslie suffered a great loss that proved to be a key aspect of the healing she received from her past life regression. In tears when she arrived at my office, Leslie relayed the following:

"My cat died last week and I can't stop crying," she explained. "When my neighbor was leaving for work he accidentally backed over him. He didn't mean to, I know that, and he apologized and offered to pay me or replace him, but you know animals can't be replaced."

So true. Although Leslie didn't initially come in to discuss her cat, her beloved pet became an unexpected focal point of her regression. Her best friend Cindy had died in a car accident only two years earlier and her cat's death brought to the forefront of her mind unresolved grief from the loss of her friend.

To begin the session, Leslie visualized meeting her friend and her cat in a room where she had a chance to talk to them both about anything that was left unsaid. After shedding tears, Leslie seemed to feel better and eventually felt ready to go into her past lives. When she did, she discovered their deep love was centuries old and that her cat had more in common with her friend's death than Leslie had originally realized:

SK: What year is this and where are you, the first thing that comes to your mind?

Leslie: I'm not sure of the year, but I'm hearing my inner voice say France.

SK: Very good. What's happening in France?

Leslie: I am a little girl. I live in a farming village. We raise animals and are happy but poor. I am part of a family with several children and my parents are in the fur trade.

SK: As you experience the energies of the people around you, is there anyone you recognize from your current lifetime?

Leslie: (After a moment) Yes. The father. He's my neighbor and…(in tears) there's Cindy. She's one of my siblings. And Sebastian. He's there too.

SK: Who?

Leslie: Sebastian is my cat. He's not a cat here though. He's one of our animals. One of those furry little things the kings and queens used in their robes. My sister and I play with him and take care of him.

SK: Fast-forward to the next most significant event in this life in France. Be there now. Notice what's happening.

Leslie: My father took our pet and sold him to someone so he would be killed for his fur. I never forgive my father. My sister and I had gone out in the fields and when we came home, our pet was gone and we never saw him again. I'm older so I confront my father; he says the animal was not for play. We cry over that and I never get over it, but my sister is more forgiving. Cindy was like that, too, in this life: kind and loving to everybody, no matter what. She was one of the good ones who passed too soon.

SK: What lessons did you learn from this experience of losing your pet and how is this affecting you in your current life?

Leslie: I became a vegetarian pretty early on in this life, even though I wasn't raised that way. I don't understand why people kill animals for their fur. It makes me sick. That's how Cindy and I connected, actually. Apparently, she felt the same way I do, and maybe this is why.

SK: What lessons are you learning with your neighbor?

Leslie: Forgiveness. I do forgive him this time, for whatever reason. It's not the same. I felt it was an accident this time. He didn't mean to run Sebastian over, I know that; but when he took my little animal way back when, that was not an accident at all.

SK: How does Sebastian's death and the loss of your pet back then relate to your relationship with Cindy in your current life?

Leslie: We all die at some point and we shouldn't blame anyone. Things happen when they're supposed to, even though we don't like it. Cindy's death was such a shock, but it taught me about grace, and to live each day to the fullest, as if it were your last.

SK: Bring your father's Higher Self out, along with the Higher Self of your neighbor, Cindy's Higher Selves from then and now, and Sebastian and the little creature from your past. Imagine that who you were then and who you are now can have a conversation with everyone and discuss all of this and what you've come here to learn as souls.

Leslie: Nobody lives forever. We have to learn a certain degree of detachment, although I became so attached to the little animal then; and in my current life Cindy was my best friend, and Sebastian has been my constant companion, especially ever since Cindy died. I need to get out more and to remember that life is short, and when it's your time there's nothing you can do about that. Even though I blamed my father in that earlier life for taking my pet, from this perspective I can see that all of us choose when we come and go. Cindy's Higher Self explained that to me in the earlier part of our session when I first talked to her. She told me she wanted to stay, but it wasn't meant to be and that I would be okay.

SK: What lessons are you learning from Cindy and Sebastian this time around?

Leslie: To love unconditionally for as long as it lasts.

SK: Can you forgive your father and neighbor?

Leslie: Yes.

I had Leslie do a cord cutting, which is basically where the client imagines there is a cord between them and the other people from the regression, and healing light is sent to the situation. In Leslie's case, once the healing light poured over everyone involved, she reported that she felt better.

When I followed up with Leslie, I mentioned that I believed the animal from her past may have been an ermine. In paintings of European monarchs from hundreds of years ago, they often have a white fur collar with black specks adorning their robes. I sent a link to Leslie and she wrote back immediately and confirmed this was what she had seen. Ermine are members of the weasel family, and while they're not exactly seen as pets, in early times, someone would have had to raise them for fur to provide to various dignitaries.[1] Her narrative seemed plausible enough. Based on what I'd learned about ermine and after speaking to Leslie, intuitively I believed there might be something to this that was quite valid indeed.

The next time I saw Leslie, she told me that rather than having another cat, she had recently adopted a puppy from a shelter in hopes that dog walking would get her out and about more so she could meet new people. She'd been taking the little pup to the local dog park and seemed much more at ease and noticeably happier, and for me, that's all that matters. Her grief had been transformed and she learned from experience that life does indeed go on after loss.

---

1. New World Encyclopedia contributors, Ermine, (*New World Encyclopedia,*) 3 October 2013 14:20 UTC, http://www.newworldencyclopedia.org/p/index.php?title=Ermine&oldid=974401.

Vet Seth Met His Cat at a Russian Circus

I met Seth the veterinarian at an expo and he stopped by my booth because he'd always been curious about his connections to his profession. He believed without a doubt that he had worked with animals in the past:

"I've always loved animals and ever since I was a kid, I knew for sure I would be a vet. I do acknowledge that I'm lucky in that regard. So many people struggle to find what they want to do in life and I've never had that problem. Still, I'm curious if I've had past lives that would help me understand why I knew so absolutely that this was my calling, and if there are more things I need to learn in the future."

Advocating for animals is a worthy cause that most of us assume originated in modern times, yet Seth discovered that part of his soul mission involved working as a sort of activist for animals in an extremely cruel environment from the deep past. He also uncovered an unexpected connection with a cat who lived at his office:

SK: Where are you and what year is this? What's happening?

Seth: Russia, 1800s. I am in a circus. Animals everywhere. I see myself center stage, directing the animals and the entertainers. I'm out on the stage, looking out at the crowd. The audience is applauding.

SK: How do you feel?

Seth: I enjoy being in front of the crowd, but I can't relax.

SK: Why not?

Seth: There's a constant fear I carry with me. I'm worried about the people in charge. They're cruel and very demanding. I do my best to take care of everyone who works for me—the people and the animals, but everything has to be perfect. Every trick has to go just right. No missed steps. If a performer misses a cue or an animal fails to jump through a hoop, for example, everyone suffers. I want us all to be safe, and at the same time, I want us all to stay alive. One false move or mistake could be the end of me, my crew, or the animals. I hate it because I am ultimately responsible for every single life out there. Because of that, I constantly look over my shoulder, praying that everything goes well, and I have to be very careful.

SK: Very good. Fast-forward to a moment that explains your current calling to be a vet.

Seth: The Russians were quite strict and saw the animals as a means of making money. I care for the animals. If there's not enough for them to eat, I take food off my own plate to feed them. There's not much food for the performers either, but there's very little for our animals. I find myself constantly sneaking around, trying to steal food for all of us. I have access to places the others don't so I do what I can to help everyone. It's tricky though. I have to sneak around a lot. If I'm caught feeding them extra food or showing favor, I could be in big trouble—punished or killed. In public I must put on a show and pretend I have no feelings, but I do.

SK: As you take a look at the energy of everyone around you in that lifetime, is there anyone there who looks or feels familiar to you in your current life?

Seth: People, no, but I do see my cat Felix. In this life, he's a stray I picked up and he lives in my office. He sits in the window and greets everybody when they come in—cats, dogs, birds, you name it. Felix is always a great host. He was there in Russia. He was a cat then, too, who used to hang around the livestock area helping us to control the rat population. Most people considered him expendable, but I fed him, too, right along with all the other animals around there.

SK: Is this the only other time you and Felix have been together?

Seth: Yes.

SK: What lessons are you and Felix learning together over the course of these two lifetimes?

Seth: Felix is here to thank me for my help and to support my soul purpose, which is to help the animals no matter what. He's kind of like a bonus. A good friend. There's no doubt he's helped me at my practice. Everybody knows Felix and they love him and he's kind of the icebreaker to help everyone relax when they first come in. Going to the vet is not always pleasant, so Felix helps my clients understand I have their best interests in mind, which of course I do. He also says he's my security guard, although I am teasing him about that now. He wouldn't hurt a fly. He never swats at any of the other animals, not ever. He greets everyone who comes into the practice as if they're a new friend and makes them feel right at home. He's a big help.

Animals are friends to many, and Seth proved that, sometimes, they come back to help us continue with our life purpose. Having a wonderful animal in your life feels like a reward for good behavior in the past, and Seth certainly found that to be the case with his dear cat.

Tessa's Divorce Became Unbearable after Her Cat Died

Tessa had several setbacks that caused her severe grief. She initially came in to see me because of her divorce. She wanted answers about the connection she and her ex shared, what lessons they came together to learn, and ideas for how she could move forward without him.

"My ex cheated on me repeatedly and I did nothing about it. I should have divorced him years ago when this first started, but I hung on. I couldn't let him go. Now he's the one who dumped me for a younger model. What's worse," she broke into tears, "my cat Alvin just died and I feel more upset about that than about my ex. Losing Alvin made me question whether I ever really loved my husband at all. I'm so angry.

I feel stupid and sad that I wasted so many years of my life on someone who obviously doesn't care about me at all."

During her regression, Tessa discovered there were deep roots between her and her ex, but that their past connection wasn't quite what she expected:

SK: Where are you and what year is this?

Tessa: Europe somewhere. Very early times.

SK: Are you a man or woman?

Tessa: I'm not sure.

SK: Imagine you can look at your feet and notice what kind of shoes you're wearing.

Tessa: (Gasps) I have boots and armor on. I'm a man!

SK: Very good. So what is happening in that life in early Europe?

Tessa: I'm in a battle fighting in my armor. I live and everyone considers me a hero.

SK: Fast-forward to another significant event in that life. Be there now. What happens next?

Tessa: I see I am in a castle in a king's court. Lots of ladies around.

SK: Anyone there you know in your current life?

Tessa: Oh yes, my ex is there. He's my wife, only I have eyes on the king's daughter and I have the audacity to have an affair with her behind everyone's backs. We get caught, though, and I am executed for the crime.

SK: What lessons did you and your ex learn about in that life that you're still learning about in your present situation?

Tessa: He's giving me a taste of my own medicine so I can experience the humiliation.

SK: You mentioned your cat. Is that an energy you've known before?

Tessa: Oh yes.

SK: Very good. Be there now and tell me what's happening.

Tessa: Alvin was also my cat during another lifetime I had in a royal court. It feels like France. I see him perched on my lap and courtiers all around me. He's spoiled and the men don't like how much attention I pay to him.

SK: As you experience the souls of those courtiers and all others in the life in France, is there anyone you know from your current life?

Tessa: Oh wow, there's my ex again. He's trying to ask for my hand in marriage, but I am busy flirting and carrying on with all the other men. He also resents my cat because I seem to like the cat more than him.

SK: Do the two of you marry in the life in France?

Tessa: Nope. I picked someone else. I further insulted him there, too, by stringing him along until the bitter end then dumping him for an older, richer man. No doubt, he got back at me this time around for that life also.

SK: Having understood all of this, would it be easier for you now to let go and forgive your ex so you can both move on?

Tessa: I never thought I'd hear myself saying this, but yes, absolutely.

SK: Are you ready to completely let this go so you won't have to come back and repeat this situation in a future life?

Tessa: Oh yes, definitely.

SK: Imagine your ex's Higher Self can come out and talk to you about these lessons. Would it be okay for the two of you to end this cyclical behavior, remain civil, and part peacefully? Imagine you can ask him if he would agree to this resolution.

Tessa: Yes.

SK: Very good. What about your cat, Alvin? What lessons did he come here to help you with in your current life and back in France?

Tessa: Alvin is a gauge. He's here to help me understand my feelings. Even in France I should have known right away that if I love my cat more than the person trying to court me, then there's no use in continuing the relationship. Back then I was too self-centered to care, and in this life, of course, I loved Alvin more. He was always there for me; he was my shoulder to cry on when my ex was out all the time. In a way, Alvin tried to warn me, but I wouldn't listen.

I see several events where the man in France keeps coming by, giving me gifts, offering to do things for me. He's practically begging for my attention, and the whole time I am fixated on Alvin. I brush his fur and coddle him, and I'm so rude I won't even make eye contact with this poor man.

I wasn't very nice back then. Money spoiled me and I didn't care about anyone else's feelings. Alvin showed me that I loved him more, but thanks to family pressure and the society, I continued with my horrible behavior and wound up marrying a richer man, but he wasn't as nice to me. After we married, I spent more time alone with Alvin until he died, then I continued married to a very cold man. I got what I deserved, I guess. The other man who is my current ex-husband would have been a better choice. Actually, I should have stayed single, but people didn't do that back in those times. Or they rarely did. I hope I've learned the lessons though. I don't want to go through this in my next life! I am grateful to little Alvin though. He helped me during some dark days.

Before the session was over, we did some more healing on the situation, adding light and a few more conversational points about specifics that related to the property they were dividing.

I spoke with Tessa some time later. She said the divorce went more smoothly than imagined and her ex actually gave her more than she had originally requested. She stopped threatening him with further lawsuits and sent him on his way, wishing him well. In the end, it turned out about as good as things could in such circumstances. This is one case that goes to show when we heal ourselves, then everyone around us changes. As for the grief she felt about losing Alvin the cat, Tessa adopted a kitten and she moved forward in peace.

Siamese Cat Was Jeff's Past Life Friend in Thailand

Jeff decided to have a past life regression after an exploratory trip of Thailand left him with more questions than answers.

"I'm glad I got to go to Thailand because it's been on my mind for years, but when I was there, I didn't feel well at all. Now that I'm home, I'm having nightmares that I think have to do with a past life. In the dreams, I'm lost in a rainforest-type environment. I'm hungry and I eat things that cause my stomach to become so ill, I find myself crawling around, praying my life will end. I did get sick while I was there, even though nobody else in my group had any problems at all. The place we stayed was clean and nice, so I don't think it had anything to do with that. When I wake up from the nightmares, I usually have a very painful stomachache, even though logically, I know the dreams aren't real.

Or are they? I've been so sick, I've had to miss some work. I even went to my doctor about this and he confirmed that I didn't have a fever or elevated white blood cells or anything to suggest infection, but he put me on some antibiotics anyway, just in case I'd caught some kind of stomach bug over there. I finished the medication over a month ago, but I'm still having the dreams, not quite as often, but at least once a week. My stomach is only a little better. I'm hoping a regression might help."

As I reported in my book *Meet Your Karma*, "last resort" is a common reason to seek a regression. With Jeff, I could certainly understand his desire to search for other possibilities rather than suffer with intestinal distress much longer. I hoped the session would help alleviate his discomfort at best, or at least provide insight into why the condition came up out of nowhere. I asked Jeff if he'd ever had stomach problems before the trip, and he said he'd never had. His reaction is similar to what I experienced in Key West years ago, which I later discovered had ties to a past life. I felt certain Jeff experienced a form of *Supretrovie*, an externally induced past life memory brought on by travel. Some of these spontaneous memories and conditions are pleasant, but unfortunately, in Jeff's case, the reaction was so bad, the situation affected his current life in a drastic way. In the session, I asked him to contact his Spirit Guide for help answering questions so we could get to the source event of the issue and see if he actually did have ties to that part of the world or if something else caused his discomfort:

> *SK:* Ask your guide if your soul lived a past life in Thailand, yes or no. Notice the first answer that pops into your mind.
>
> *Jeff:* Yes.
>
> *SK:* Very good. Imagine you and your guide can float there now. Go way, way, way back and be there now. Notice what's happening. Where are you?
>
> *Jeff:* In a jungled area in Thailand. Not too far from where I went on my trip.
>
> *SK:* Very good. When is this? What year? The first thing that comes to your mind.
>
> *Jeff:* (Hesitating) A thousand comes to mind.
>
> *SK:* Like 1000 BC?

Jeff: Yes.

SK: Very good. So what's happening there? Are you a man or a woman? Fast-forward through your life and notice what it's like there.

Jeff: Man. I live in the woods as part of a small group of people. We live off the land. I am about twenty or so. We do fairly well, but then there's bad weather. Not enough rain one year and our food is diminished so we are forced to eat things we normally wouldn't. I become gravely ill and eventually die.

SK: Float into the peaceful space between lives. Be there now. What lessons did you learn during that life?

Jeff: Nothing lasts. You have to be resourceful.

SK: How did this past life affect you in your current life? What's the reason?

Jeff: I shouldn't have had a problem, but somehow I picked up on that energy when I was there.

SK: Can you be free of that energy now?

Jeff: Yes.

We did a cord cutting to disconnect Jeff from the unwanted energy of that past life and brought healing light into his stomach.

SK: Let me know when this feels better.

Jeff: Yes, much better.

SK: As you experience the energy of the other people from that time, is there anyone you know in your current life?

Jeff: (Laughing) My cat Brownie's there. He's back with me this time. He's one of the reasons I wanted to go to Thailand.

SK: What lessons are you and Brownie learning in these lives together?

Jeff: To look out for one another. He lived in that same area where I was and we hunted together. I never tried killing him and he never attacked me either. We helped each other then and we still help each other now. He showed up on my porch one day and never left. He found me for a reason to help me heal from that past life. I know that now.

SK: What kind of cat is he?

Jeff: Siamese. When he first showed up, I knew nothing about them and that's when I found out that Siamese cats are from Thailand. That started me thinking about the trip. Although back then, he was much larger, more of a predator, like a panther. I'm glad he didn't kill me and have me for dinner back then. He could have easily enough.

Once we finished Jeff's past life regression, I had him progress to a future memory where his stomach issues were a thing of the past:

SK: Be there now. What year is this and what's happening?

Jeff: It's a few months from now.

SK: How do you feel?

Jeff: I see myself watching TV with Brownie. We're there chilling out together like we always do. My stomach feels fine and I can sense I haven't had any more nightmares.

After the session, Jeff promised to keep in touch and let me know how it was going. He wrote several months later to say the session worked, his stomach hadn't given him any issues since we'd met, and he still enjoyed the companionship of his buddy, Brownie the Siamese cat.

Melissa Repaid a Past Life Debt to Her Cat

Anyone who fosters and helps animals is an angel in my book. Melissa had been volunteering with her local animal shelter for years, but her love of pets had nothing to do with her desire to have a past life regression. She came to ask about her family after her mother died of cancer. She had questions and wanted to know if there was anything she could do from a spiritual perspective to clear herself energetically so she would not suffer the same fate.

One of the more interesting kinds of regressions I sometimes do involves taking people into the past lives of their ancestors. Believe it or not, you can actually travel back in time down your mother's and father's ancestral lines and do clearings that can have broad healing effects on your whole family. After working with Melissa's mother's line, we were not able to come up with anything conclusive other than the message that her mother had certain life lessons to experience that did not directly affect Melissa, so the next step was to go into her own past lives to see if there were any proactive courses of action she could find and adapt.

"I want to make sure there's nothing in my past lives that might trigger me to become ill later on because I've heard this kind of cancer runs in families. So far, my doctors don't seem to think I have any predispositions toward it since I take after my dad. Still, I want to be sure there's nothing lingering out there. I want to be around for my kids. I hope if I go at this from a spiritual perspective to see why this showed up in my path I can figure out if there's anything I can do to change things or make new decisions."

Melissa shared my belief that our souls are here to learn and grow and that it's possible we made many of our life choices before we arrived in our current lifetimes. The Higher Self and soul can choose new decisions based on what we've already learned. From that perspective, Melissa traveled back into a difficult life on the American frontier:

SK: What year is this and where are you in the world?

Melissa: Mid-1800s. I'm in a wagon train on the Oregon Trail. I've always known I was part of this experience.

SK: What's happening?

Melissa: We're in terrible conditions, bad weather, storms, there's very little food. Several people don't make it and I see myself as a young teenage girl helping out with my mother by my side. She's reminding me to be strong.

SK: As you experience the energy of your mother in that life, is she anyone you know in your current lifetime?

Melissa: Oh yes. It's my mom from this life.

SK: Very good. How did your time in the wagon train affect your current life? Fast-forward through the events and notice what's happening.

Melissa: We're enduring unbelievably difficult conditions. My mother is very ill and there's not much food. She's making sure I get more than she does because she tells me she's not going to make it. I see myself crying, begging her to eat, but she won't. She sacrifices herself to save me. Once she's gone, I help to care for everyone else, including the horses and other animals. There are dogs and even a few cats. One of the cats keeps me company and even sleeps with me, although I don't let anyone around me know that. He's a true comfort and helps ease my grief. I share my food with all the animals, but this one cat has a special place in my heart.

   When I look into his eyes, I can see he's one of my rescues, Simon, whom I acquired a few years back and ended up adopting. He's passed on now in this life, but he was such a blessing to me. He came around right at the time my mom got sick and stayed with me through her death, and was a big part of my grieving process. I couldn't have made it without him.

I can see now that he's the same cat I knew back then, and if it wasn't for him and his companionship, I wouldn't have made it. I owed him. Because of this experience and how my mom taught me to be in both lifetimes—to be of service, to always try to help those who are less fortunate—that's why I love the animals so much now. Even in this current life. My mom was a big part of that. I owe her a debt of gratitude and I also owe all the animals who have loved me and helped me get through tough times.

SK: Do you make it to Oregon or wherever you're headed?

Melissa: I do. I see myself on a homestead raising lots of animals, livestock, chickens, cattle, horses, and of course, I always have cats and dogs. The cat who helped me on the trail passes, but the kittens that came from him and another female continue to live with me for as long as I remain there. That's why I still love Oregon so much and decided to come back here in this lifetime. My mom chose this life, too, so she could experience the place that she didn't quite make it to in the earlier days. We had a mission then and now. One other interesting thing is that Simon, my cat, had a litter of kittens with one of my other females and some of those kitties are still with me now, similar to how things were back then.

SK: Regarding your own health, do you see anything from this situation that needs to be cleared or changed?

Melissa: No. I have to accept things day by day. I am going to be fine. My mother had a different lesson to learn through her illness and we came together so she could teach me how to be strong on my own. A lot of that has to do with my animals, particularly that one cat. I owe him and I still repay him and all the other animals by helping them out now. That's also how I honor my mother's memory. Life has ups and downs, but everything will work out.

Melissa is a special soul who has a razor-sharp clarity about her mission in life and that is amazing to see. We need people like her in this world who are willing to help others despite their own needs, and Melissa is certainly one of those earth angels. I know her mother would be proud.

Chad Knew His Cat from a Ukrainian Farm

Chad worked in corporate America after being raised on a dairy farm in Iowa run by several generations of his family. When he chose a life other than farming, his father, in particular, was not at all pleased.

"Farming is not for everybody," Chad explained. "It's a hard life, a solitary kind of life, and I wanted something different. I went to college, got a degree in business, and went into sales and marketing. I'm around a lot of people and I enjoy my work, but I still struggle with the relationship problems with my dad, and I wish I could go back and see if there's something besides this life that's giving us trouble. He's not in great health, and I need to help him make amends with me before he leaves. I don't want bad karma!"

Chad seemed nice enough and clearly he had made an effort where his father was concerned, so I couldn't imagine him racking up bad karma from his actions, but still, we ventured into the past where he and his father had lived before:

SK: Where are you?

Chad: Ukraine?

SK: What year is this?

Chad: 1367.

SK: Very good. What's happening in the Ukraine in 1367?

Chad: I'm on a farm. We grow grain and live off the land. I am older. I have a wife and a few kids.

SK: As you experience the energy of your family, anyone there feel familiar to you?

Chad: Yes. My dad is there. He's one of my sons. I also see we have feral cats wandering around and one of those looks like my cat Toby. I just adopted him from a shelter. I've always had cats ever since I moved away from the farm. They're nice and quiet pets and easy to take care of in cities. My dad never understood why I liked them. He constantly nags me for that.

SK: Forward through events in your life in Ukraine and notice some of the things that happen there and how those may be affecting you now.

Chad: My son grows up and stays and helps me with the farm. He does everything, actually, and as I age, he takes care of me. He has a real gift for the farm that I don't. I only got into farming because my father did it and there were no other options.

SK: How does this situation affect your relationship in your current life?

Chad: On some level, my dad believes I owe him; not only because of how he raised me this time, but for what he did for me back then. I am grateful to him, but farming's not for me. I can't help that.

SK: Bring the Higher Selves of your son from your life in Ukraine and your dad out and imagine you can speak to them. Let them know how you feel, that you're grateful, but this is not for you; see if they can come to an understanding at a soul level and forgive you. Take your time, let me know when this is finished.

Chad: Okay, they both say they get it. They understand. The farming is in their soul, they're saying.

SK: Bring your cat Toby out also. What lessons are you learning with Toby, and how is Toby affecting your life with your dad?

Chad: Dad sees the cats as pieces of equipment, like they have jobs to do, which involves keeping the farm free of rodents and pests. He can't see them as pets. Even in Ukraine, it was my wife that showed me how to take care of them and be kind to them so they would stick around and be helpful, and I came to really enjoy their company. I hated it when a larger predator got to one of them, and I carried this love of cats into my current life. My son in that life didn't see it that way. He thought of the cats as another thing he needed to take care of, like they were a burden. I never saw cats as anything but allies. I'm connected to them. Dad will never get that because his attitude toward them is the same as it was back then. Dad's old now and he isn't going to change, but that's okay. I can accept him anyway.

Chad had an imaginary conversation with his dad where they talked about many aspects of their relationship. When you do these kinds of exercises in your mind, real healing can transpire on the physical plane. The results can be quite miraculous because even though all of this takes place in the realm of the imagination; the person receiving healing gets it on some level.

I heard from Chad a while later and asked if things with his dad were any better. He reported that from what he could see, things hadn't changed much in terms of how his dad perceived him. His father was aging and becoming quite set in his ways, but Chad did notice that his own attitude about the situation had improved and he'd come to a greater sense of acceptance about the underlying feelings that informed the situation, and by understanding that, he felt far more peaceful moving forward. Chad believed that his dad could feel fairly good about him and the relationship as he transitioned into his next life.

Summing Up

One of the most interesting aspects of these regressions is how surprised everyone seems at finding the connection with their cat. This feeling continues for other animal lovers as well. Even I was surprised when I did my regression to uncover the source of my love for my cat BisKit.

Later in part two, you will have a chance to have such experiences yourself. For now, let's take a look at more surprises in store for the people who realized their connection to man's best friend proved far deeper than they had originally thought.

Chapter Two

PAST LIVES WITH DOGS

DOGS INSPIRE GREAT LOVE and loyalty, and that will be affirmed in the next several case studies. I have mainly owned cats throughout my current life, but I now consider myself to be a dog lover. Although that was not always the case.

In my earlier book *Meet Your Karma*, I very briefly described a phobia I developed after I was attacked by a dog at the age of four. I was playing on a swing set when, in a flash, the dog rushed over and had my head in his mouth. He did extensive damage before the adults stopped him. I still have faint scars where he bit off a chunk of my nose, and I can still see the indented tooth mark in the side of my left temple.

Thanks to my young age, I remember very little about the actual event. Even so, I have been deathly afraid of dogs my current whole life. After working with myself on a cognitive level, I eventually received a past life regression where I went back to a life in the 1200s in an icy environment in what would now be northern Scandinavia. I worked alongside a gigantic white long-haired dog with big brown eyes that was akin to a modern-day Samoyed. Strangely, when I was a kid, even after the incident with the dog attack, I had a stuffed white Samoyed toy. Apparently, my soul was drawn to the ancient remembrance of my past life pet. Several brief visions passed before my eyes of many lifetimes where dogs were around me, yet I could not find any negative lives with dogs at all.

When asked what lessons I had learned by having the dog bite me in this lifetime, I said the dog attack helped me learn to overcome adversity and to be stronger in all areas of life.

My regression really helped me by showing me the depth of love I hold for dogs and by demonstrating quite clearly that past life regression works wonders in healing this type of situation. I began doing regressions for others because of the vast benefits I've received from them myself. For me, there is no better way to heal from any life issues than by doing regression. I hope you will find regression works for you too.

People cope with reality the best they can and often such traumas get pushed so far back in our minds that we forget to do anything about them. This is because our subconscious mind hides them away to try to keep us safe. We push away things that might be amazing experiences when we hold on to unresolved fear, and yet we do the best we can.

I still believe all things happen in their time. The good news is that I now actually seek out dogs. My entire vibration has changed around them, and I can now fully appreciate the loyal and loving qualities of the canine species as I did in my past lives.

The following case histories prove that while I am not the only person who has dog issues, most of the clients I've worked with love the loyal companionship of man's best friend.

Jill Feared Separation from Her Beloved Poodle

Divorce is a nasty business. Even under the best circumstances someone is bound to get their feelings hurt and misunderstandings prevail. Once the legal proceedings end, couples can often get past their pain and go on to be friends. Relationship insights are always a big reason for people to seek regression, and Jill was no exception. She and her ex, Scott, got along fine and the divorce seemed to be going smoothly other than where their dog was concerned:

"Scott's been so good about everything. I'm keeping the main house, he's taking our vacation home, and everything else is getting divided equally; but he's digging his heels in on our dog Zoey, and no matter what I say, he won't give in. He bought her for me for my birthday, so I don't know why he wants her other than to punish me for wanting the divorce. It's ridiculous! He's a bodybuilder. What would he want with a poodle? I love Scott. I always will, but we've changed. We married so young and now it's like I'm getting new interests and he's stuck in the past. I truly want the best for him, but without Zoey, I won't make it. She's my constant companion. I want to know what past life connections Scott and I have to see if I can talk him into giving me the thing I want the most."

Zoey the poodle turned out to be the only point of contention in an otherwise relatively civil dissolution of Jill's marriage. We did the regression to see what links she and Scott had from the past that could be healed at a deeper level, and Jill found some surprising information about them both:

SK: Where are you and what year is this?

Jill: 1400s in northern Europe. I want to say Germany, but we didn't call it that back then. I live on a giant estate. I'm the wife of a landowner and we have lots of people working the land, selling the food we grow off to others.

SK: Very good. When you experience that energy on your land and the people you're with, is there anyone there you know from your current life?

Jill: Oh yes. Scott's there. He's my husband.

SK: Good job. How does that relationship from the past relate to the one you're having in your current life?

Jill: He's similar now. He loves me so much and he would do anything for me. He's a good provider. I see Zoey there too. In that life, she was a larger poodle. She was one of his hunting dogs and helped him in the fields, although she and I formed an attachment, so he allowed her to come into our home and I cared for her until we started having children. Once the kids arrived, he took her back outside. I was upset, but the kids took a lot of my time.

SK: After he removed her from the home, what happened to your dog back then?

Jill: She was shot during a hunting trip. It was heartbreaking. My husband says he didn't do it, but I never believed him. It was an accident of course, but still, I blamed him for taking her from me.

SK: How does this situation come into play now in your current life and what lessons are the two of you learning about as souls?

Jill: It's strange, but the kids thing is one of our biggest issues now. He wants them, I don't. I want to work on my career, travel, and have fun. That's the main reason we can't stay together anymore, even though we've dated since high school and had always planned on growing old together. Things changed. Looking at this lifetime, I can see here that I resented having my kids because my husband took my dog away from me. I thought I should have both, but he didn't see things that way. To him, the kids were everything.

Allowing the dog into our home was unusual in the first place, but I wish he'd never done it because it caused me a lot of heartache. Now he wants to take her to get back at me for not having kids and I'm afraid if he does, she won't survive. Zoey has always been my dog first, and I just want to make sure she's happy and well cared-for during her lifetime. Not that he'd be mean to her. He loves her, too, but she belongs with me.

We did a huge healing on all of this and I had Jill speak to Scott's Higher Self from the earlier life in Germany. She forgave him for taking her dog and for indirectly causing her dog's death. She also talked to Scott's Higher Self from the current life, thanking him for the time they had together and they came to peace about wanting different things in life. Once that healing happened, she asked him if he would be willing to give Zoey back to her.

When people go into their minds to do healing work like this, it all appears to be born solely of the imagination, but incredible healing can and often does happen as a result. In Jill's case, after our session and further real-life discussions with her soon-to-be ex, Scott admitted he wanted the family pickup truck, which Jill had planned to keep. She had no idea he liked it since she'd purchased it years earlier and it was not worth much in terms of value. Once they arrived at that understanding, Scott willingly gave Zoey to her.

"I thought he'd want to at least come and see Zoey from time to time," she told me when I next saw her, "but he never did. In fact, I heard he's engaged to someone else now, and I'm fine with that. I hope they're happy and he gets the kids he's always wanted."

Relationships provide us with the greatest learning experiences in our lives. Life brings hard lessons when we grow apart from someone we've known for a long time. Expectations for what we thought our lives should be must change and, at times, the best course of action for growth is to say goodbye and move forward into the future to await what's next. Opening your hands to the possibilities and moving forward in life when you're meant to part ways with souls from the past can be quite transformational. In Jill's case, she moved forward with a great love of her life—her dog Zoey.

Buddy Helped Charlie Escape Past Life Prison

Charlie came to see me to help figure out his soul purpose and see if he was doing the right kind of work. He had a great career but felt there was something else he would be more suited for and hoped that by traveling into his past lives, he could discover more about his ideal profession. A side issue he mentioned was that he'd been having horrible nightmares about being trapped and unable to move. He believed that the dream might be telling him something and that feeling contributed to the idea that he was stuck in his job. He tried writing down notes after awakening, but the dream only went so far, then ended. He hoped past life regression might help.

"In the dream, I'm stuffed into a really small space. It's hot, it smells, and I can't break free. It's like a feeling of terrible claustrophobia, although I've never experienced anything like that ever before. I wonder if this is a message that I need to make a change."

Dreams definitely inform our daily life and can offer clues about our past lives. Sometimes an old memory can surface at a time in life that corresponds to the same age certain things happened in the past. Clearly something important was trying to come through, but what? In his mid-thirties, Charlie never married and had just received a promotion as a construction foreman. The current project happened to be a low-security prison. I asked if these dreams happened recently or how long they'd been going on.

"I hadn't thought of that before, but yeah, the dreams started about the time I got this promotion, and shortly after that we began working on the new job. I'm making a lot more money now as foreman, but without sleep, I'm beginning to think it isn't worth it, plus I don't know how this is helping anybody. I need to know my life has meaning."

The job would only last a year, maybe less, but Charlie needed sleep and peace of mind in order to keep going. His regression proved quite informative:

SK: Where are you and what year is this?

Charlie: I want to say 1799. I'm on a ship, stuffed inside a really cramped space with hundreds of other people. It's hot and the stench is awful. I'm nauseous just thinking about it.

SK: Very good. Fast-forward through this situation and notice whether or not you arrive to your destination.

Charlie: After what seems like months, yes, I do make it, but a lot of people didn't survive.

SK: Very good. Be there now. Notice what's happening.

Charlie: We've finally reached land. I see them pulling the ship up to the shore. There's nothing around anywhere. Once they get it tied off, the men in charge come to get us. They're shouting and hitting us if we don't hurry up. We're all being marched out of the ship shackled together in chains. I'm a prisoner.

SK: Where did you come from? Imagine you can remember.

Charlie: England.

SK: Continue to notice what happens after they take you off the ship. Be there now.

Charlie: We're marching single file from the shore inland. Some of the men don't make it and die on the way. Eventually they put us in brick buildings. We're crammed in there with other people who were there before us, and the conditions are terrible. I'm starving and several of the people around me are getting sick and dying.

SK: Imagine you can ask your Spirit Guide where you're at and why you're subjected to all of this.

Charlie: I'm hearing Australia. Ah, no wonder I've never wanted to go there. I am a criminal and they transported me here to spend out my life.

SK: Very good. What crime did you commit to get there? Imagine you can remember back to what caused you to receive this punishment.

Charlie: I have a family and now I'll never see them again. We are so poor, practically starving, and living in bad conditions. I stole something to eat. Like bread or something. To feed my family.

Now I can't help them at all. There's no mercy and now I'm paying the price. Every day I worry that they're stuck in England and likely starving. If they try to steal food like I did, they'll receive the same fate, maybe worse.

SK: Very good. Now fast-forward through your life in prison and notice what happens. Do you ever get out?

Charlie: Actually I do. There's a wild dog wandering outside my cell. The place I'm kept has wooden bars and I start sharing my food with him. He gnaws on my cage and helps me break free. I'm running to safety thanks to him, and we go away from everyone and try to survive off the land. The conditions there are so harsh though, it's tough. But I do manage, thanks to the dog.

SK: As you experience the energy of all the souls you encountered during this life in Australia, is there anyone there you know in your current life?

Charlie: Yes, the owner of the construction firm where I work was there. We were friends in prison, but unfortunately, he passed away. I always liked him and we were friends the moment we met in this life. He's a big reason why I stay where I am rather than look elsewhere. He's a good guy. He'd also had a family and was sent to Australia for stealing food.

SK: Good job. Anyone else?

Charlie: Yeah, Buddy, my dog. I got him from the animal shelter; from a prison of sorts not too long ago. He was the dingo that helped me in Australia. He's part of the reason why I've had the dreams. The prison project also made me remember. I can see why I had to do the prison construction now, because otherwise, I would never have known about this past life.

SK: What lessons are you and Buddy learning together as souls?

Charlie: Freedom is in your mind first. And friendship. He's a loyal friend. So is my boss.

SK: How does this lifetime relate to your soul purpose, or does it?

Charlie: I'm extremely good at building things and I learned how to do much of that when I was in Australia. Later in my life, once I broke free, I had to build my own home and learn how to sterilize and contain water. I have the skills and I am using the right skills. I think it's more about what I am building rather than the building itself. I am in the right place, but I don't have the right project yet, although I can't really say that either because I've learned a lot about myself from building the prison.

We did a major healing on Charlie's trauma and traveled into his future where he saw himself still working beside his friend, only they were building schools rather than prisons. Charlie said he felt better about those projects and continued to grow within the company.

After the session, he emailed me later to say his nightmares had ended and he could more peacefully complete his work project. Thanks to karma and the Universe, it wasn't too surprising to see Charlie working on a prison complex in his current life.

Our Higher Selves present lots of scenarios to us throughout our lives to help us bring up past issues and heal, and last I heard, that's exactly what Charlie has managed to do with the help of Buddy the dog. They helped each other out of tough situations and remained loyal companions for life.

Misty's Past Life Poodle Turned Golden

Misty came to see me to help understand the terrible conflicts she'd been having at the office. She claimed she did exemplary work, yet conflicts with coworkers and her boss over minuscule and seemingly insignificant details made her life beyond difficult.

"I've been with my company for two years now and I've done my best to be positive and get my job done accurately and on time. I do a lot of detailed data entry and written communications for our customers. When my part of a document is finished, I pass it on to another coworker to continue until the completed project is passed on to our manager. We work in a team so I am an earlier link in the chain to get a project finished. I don't always work with the same exact people, which is even stranger because several of my teammates nitpick my documents, criticize my word choice and even my sentence structure, but rather than telling me about their recommendations to my face, they'd rather go to the boss.

Over time, this resulted in several instances of me being called in to explain myself. I don't know why they have it out for me. I've never met any of them before going to work there. I've never been anything but supportive to them, but now it seems like even my boss is on their side. The other day, he actually wrote me up and put that into my personnel file. I'm afraid if something doesn't change soon, I'll be out of a job. I'm wondering if there's something I could do to heal this situation before it goes too far. Despite all this, I actually enjoy the company and I don't want to leave."

During her regression, Misty traveled back to a former life, chosen by her Higher Self, that would best assist her in rectifying the situation at work:

SK: Where are you?

Misty: France.

SK: Very good. What's happening in France?

Misty: I am the daughter of a wealthy landowner in France. Because of our station in society, our family has to make a lot of appearances before the king at court.

SK: Go ahead and fast-forward to a time when you're at court. As you glance around, do you notice anyone there who you know in your current life, yes or no?

Misty: Yes. One of the palace maids is a coworker. Actually, now that I think of it, I see several of the household staff who work at the palace are the people from my current job. And the king is our boss.

SK: Very good. How does your relationship with the palace staff and king relate to your current dilemma at work?

Misty: These palace workers are jealous of me and they don't understand why I get preferential treatment at court. They gossip behind my back and spread false rumors about me, telling everyone that I am born too low to deserve everything I'm getting. They're teasing me about my parents, even though I have no control over who my family is or why I have a higher station in life.

SK: Bring their Higher Selves out to talk to your Higher Self. Imagine you can talk to them and see if you can work this situation out on a soul level. Ask them if they can explain more about why they've treated you like this and ask them if there's anything you can do to change their minds about you.

Misty: They're saying they just don't like me. I'm saying encouraging things to them, but they don't care. I'm smiling and being nice, but they say there's nothing I can do to help.

SK: What about the king? Bring his Higher Self in and see if you can work with him.

Misty: He is mainly concerned with keeping his own stress levels low. I see that his feelings about these people haven't changed much, even in our current situation. It's not that he dislikes me. He dislikes the stress and drama. He calls me into his office this time around just to save face and reduce his own stress levels. He wants the ladies to stop their complaining, and if they won't do it on their own, at some point, he would have no choice but to be rid of me. I am seeing in the past life, the staff complained about me and the king got wind of that. In that lifetime, because our family had some power, he had to take action against his staff and some of them lost their jobs because of me. That's also causing stress in the current situation, but in that life he couldn't touch me. In our office, there are more of them than of me, and he's afraid of a lawsuit if he terminates them without cause. They've given him a lot of reasons to get rid of me, and I haven't helped. I haven't stood up for myself very well.

SK: Any way to remedy this?

Misty: If I could, I would. I can't do it alone though. I could try to be more assertive and let him know that they are unnecessarily criticizing me, or I could ask for more training in the areas he says aren't up to par.

SK: Very good. As you experience the energy of that life in France, is there anyone else there who you know in your current life? Yes or no?

Misty: Yes, my poodle. He's a breath of fresh air. My father in that life bought him for me and strangely, he's another reason everybody at my work hates me. My dog is my constant companion, even at court, and he makes the housekeepers feel I am spoiled and entitled. I don't think that's a fair assessment, but I don't have any way to change their minds about me. He's the same dog I have in my current life, only this time, he's come back as my golden retriever named Doodle. My husband just bought him for me this past Christmas.

SK: You mentioned the dog being a sore spot. Do your friends at work know about your dog?

Misty: Oh yes. I have a picture of my husband and Doodle on my desk, and one of them made a snide remark about how expensive it is to get a breed dog.

SK: Thinking of the energy of your father in France, is he anyone you know in your current life?

Misty: Yes, my husband.

SK: What lessons are you and your husband working on in many lifetimes?

Misty: We get along well. We're good partners actually. We enjoy each other's company and have the ability to share a lasting relationship that is stable and peaceful. I grew up in foster care during this current life and my husband has been the one person to give me the stable home life I've always wanted. I can see I chose him because of who he was in the past.

We have a strong connection and the deep feeling of safety he brings to my life makes me feel like I can do anything. He's got my back, and it's awesome. The people at work see what we have when he comes by the office. He always sends flowers, he picks me up for lunch once in a while when he's caught up at work. Sometimes now he brings the dog.

We are happy together and this is another cause for jealousy, but I don't care. Everybody can be happy if they look within their own lives. I don't need to feel guilty for finding happiness after a rough start. I'll do my best to sort things out with my coworkers, but if that doesn't happen, I'll be okay with moving on.

I showed Misty some exercises where she could actively send blessings and healing light to the difficult people at work to see if that might help shift the energy between them. Praying for others, or sending them blessings, often creates tangible changes in the outer world, as you've seen with some of the earlier case studies. I call this healing the part of you that's someone else. We are all connected, so when you reach out to the Higher Self of another soul and bring feelings of love, peace, and harmony to them, not only do you benefit, but the other person will also receive the healing.

I've seen many miracles using this process over the years, so as with many of my clients, I recommended it to Misty, who said she would try what I suggested and see what happened. Later in the book, I will take you through a process where you can try a version of this for yourself.

Her regression reminds us that you can do the right thing, you can extend friendship and the proverbial olive branch to people in your life, but if they're not willing to change or meet you halfway, things won't always work out. I spoke to Misty a few months after our session. She did go to her boss and tried to stand her ground, and even offered to take some courses to help her improve. Although that helped a little, after the situation failed to improve, she decided to actively seek out new employment before she was forced to leave.

Misty proved that while we all have challenges to overcome in our lives, not all relationships are challenging and difficult. The connection she found with her husband provided a real blessing in her life, a sort of reward for her difficult childhood. She definitely had an open and loving attitude about others that I think we could all learn from. Our souls often seek out helpful people and pets from the past who provided us with unconditional love and stability. Misty used her regression to deepen her understanding of a wonderful connection she's had through the ages with her husband and dog.

Timothy Remembered the San Francisco Quake

A pillar of his community, Timothy had a corporate job but worked part time as a volunteer fireman. When he came to see me for a past life regression, he did so out of curiosity, and one question he had above all else— he wondered why he was so attracted to the idea of being a fireman:

"Ever since I can remember, I've wanted to be a fireman. I had toy trucks when I was a kid and anytime anyone asked, that's what I said I was gonna do. I had everything mapped out, but then during my junior year of high school, I injured my leg playing football and had to have a rod put in. That ruined my chances of being a fireman. I'm just glad I get to volunteer, but I've always wondered why I was so sure this was my calling. The job I have now is fine, but I'm still disappointed I couldn't make firefighting my full-time career. I'm wondering if some bad karma stopped me from that, or if it's just some coincidence."

Timothy found answers when he went back to a past life that wasn't very long ago:

SK: What year is this and where are you? Notice what's happening.

Timothy: San Francisco, early 1900s. There's a huge fire. Screaming, crying, and running; lots of people dying and injured. I'm frantically trying to help. I work as a firefighter and I'm at the station when we feel the ground rumbling and the fires start. I'm with a few others who also work there, but when we go out into the streets, we can't get through very well. Buildings and roads are demolished. It's complete chaos.

SK: Continue to move through your life in San Francisco and notice how it all unfolds.

Timothy: We eventually manage to make our way around our area, but we never get too far. We do save some people, but the structural damage is bad. I want to say this is the big earthquake.

SK: Continue forward in time. Do you survive the fires and earthquake?

Timothy: Yes, but I can see I did get injured pretty bad. It's weird, but the injury is on the same leg where I had the pin put in during my current life. Once I'm injured, I'm still able to fight fires, but I can't help in all situations like I used to. I'm eventually assigned to a more administrative kind of duty, but I mostly spend my time helping people rebuild their homes and repair damage from the quake.

SK: Why did you choose to be a firefighter then and now?

Timothy: This is my purpose, and I'm also paying back for something I did.

SK: What was that? Rewind in time and be there now.

Timothy: I'm in a straw-thatched roof building. Maybe Europe, but I don't see when exactly. Early. I want to say before the Middle Ages.

SK: What's happening?

Timothy: I get in a fight about something stupid. A woman and a guy are egging me on about my land. I'm very poor. I get angry and I light the guy on fire.

SK: How?

Timothy: There's a flame burning in this pub or wherever we are and I grab a stick from the pit and catch his shirt on fire. I didn't mean for him to be burned so badly though. I had a temper and lost control for a minute. Unfortunately, he goes up in a flash, screaming and burning, along with everybody else.

SK: Do you live?

Timothy: Yes, but I've got extensive scarring. In fact, I can see now why I have a lump on the skin in my chest. My family has wondered about that ever since I was a kid. We've had it tested, biopsied even, and there's nothing to it. It's just a small lump, but it happened back then.

SK: Were you punished for lighting that fire?

Timothy: Oh yes, they hung me.

SK: Be there now. Notice what's happening during these last moments of life, then find yourself lifting up, up, up, out of that life, into the peaceful space in between lives. Be there now. What lessons did you learn?

Timothy: I spent some time in limbo after that. In a space that isn't like what westerners would call hell, but it's a place where the soul goes to sit and ponder. While I was there, I made a vow to help with fires.

SK: Was your current life and San Francisco the only time you helped with fires between then and now?

Timothy: No, but I don't need to know what the other times were. I'm hearing that is not important. What is important is to save lives, not take them. Respect life.

SK: Imagine you can bring forward the Higher Self of the man you burned and apologize to him. Do that now, let me know whether or not he's willing to accept the apology.

Timothy: Okay, I'm done, and he forgives me. He said he chose to experience this situation for part of his purpose.

SK: As you consider the energy of all the souls you knew back in that early time, imagine they can also come forward and you can apologize to everyone there. Let me know what happens and when you're finished.

Timothy: Okay. They all said they chose this as souls and they forgive me.

SK: Very good. Go ahead now and notice if that man you burned is anyone you know in your current life?

Timothy: Yes, he's one of the captains across town. I know him, but not too well. He's helping others who suffer from fires. He wanted to be burned so he could have a memory that he uses now to help people. He is still letting me know it's all good.

SK: Go ahead now and float back to your life in San Francisco. Be there now in those same events, surrounded by light. Fast-forward to the last day of your life at that time and notice how it is you pass into spirit.

Timothy: Several years pass. Our station is short a man one day so I respond to a fire in a small two-story wood house. I go upstairs to help someone. I'm carrying him out when I trip on the stairs and break my leg. The same leg I injured earlier in that life and also in my current life. I am in unbelievable pain, but I manage to get the victim out, and he lives, but I got a blast of smoke in my lungs and my leg is bad. I die awhile later of internal bleeding and smoke inhalation.

SK: Floating into that peaceful space in between lives, allow the healing light to wash away your pain.

Timothy: I didn't mind the pain. I think I wanted to die in a fire to learn more about my purpose. I'm okay and that was meant to be. I helped someone and I'm good with that.

SK: Think back to your life and notice now if there's anyone else you know in your current life who was with you as a firefighter in San Francisco.

Timothy: Yes, Speckles was there, but he doesn't actually belong to me personally. He's a dalmatian who lives at the station with us. He was born to help with fires and he's been an amazing friend; not just to me but to everybody.

SK: How do these events relate to your soul purpose?

Timothy: I was meant to learn about fires, to help people. That doesn't necessarily mean I have to do that full time. Being a good person is more important, and the intent to serve.

Events that seem like mere coincidence are always packed with life lessons. I believe all souls make plans before they arrive into each lifetime, as Timothy found out when he discovered the vow he made to fight fires. Regarding the dog, Timothy explained that his firehouse in San Francisco also had a dalmatian, symbolic for firemen for over a century. Animals come in with soul purposes also, and in the case of Speckles, he shared Timothy's purpose to fight fires. In Timothy's session he explained that even Speckles chose to come back with some of his old friends from the past to pick up where they left off. Timothy felt more at ease about why he chose the path he did and he understood why the fireman's career didn't need to be a full-time endeavor for him anymore, but it was still important for his soul to consider as he moved forward in helping his fellow man during his lifetime.

Greyhound Rescue Lived with Vanessa in Ancient Times

Vanessa loved greyhound dogs her whole life, probably because her family often went to the races during her childhood. Vanessa spent much of her time during her formative years with her grandparents, and unfortunately, her grandfather's addictive behavior (in his case, gambling and smoking) rubbed off on Vanessa: She had a pack-a-day smoking habit. A recent health scare that turned out benign caused her to want to quit for good.

Stereotypically, smoking cessation and hypnotherapy seem to go hand in hand. Smoking cessation isn't something I've done much of in my practice. The multidimensional reasons people start smoking in the first place are extremely complex. Smoking can be a tactile experience where the user enjoys the actual process of smoking, the nicotine is obviously addictive, and sometimes the behavior is linked to memories from the past.

People don't always want to stop smoking for themselves; they usually want to quit for other people. I've found quitting due to family or peer pressure doesn't work as well as when someone quits for themselves, for the right reasons. I tell potential clients I'd be happy to work with them as long as they keep a journal for a week and write down every single time they smoke, where they're at, and exactly what they're doing. So much of human behavior is subconscious that unless people start to wake up and view themselves in action by consciously observing their behaviors, hypnotherapy alone may not work.

Under the right circumstances, hypnosis can be just what the person needs to help bring them to a point of internal strength where they're ready and willing to quit, but it takes effort on the client's part to make it work.

Vanessa definitely had an emotional attachment to the fun times she had with her grandfather and that had a lot to do with why she started smoking. Those memories were pleasant and she associated smoking with deep-rooted memories from childhood. Vanessa's health scare affected her enough that she wanted to take the process seriously and do her best to stop.

She was more than willing to keep a journal for me for five days and she handed it to me before our session. The journal reveals patterns such as when the smoking happens, what the mindset is when the client craves the cigarette, and other telling details that can be helpful in letting go of the addiction. You can't fix things you aren't aware of, so the simple process of becoming more conscious can be invaluable to the success of the process. During our time together, Vanessa shared more about her grandfather and how she became interested in dog rescue:

"My grandpa was a big gambler and took us to the track all the time. My sister and I would hang around and watch the races while he betted and smoked. I was around the smoke all the time. It was natural to us. Our grandma smoked, too, only not as much as grandpa. She wasn't a huge racing fan, but even she'd go along once in a while and place a bet. I still remember watching them and thinking about how grown up they looked when they smoked. They always dressed up and looked so sophisticated.

That's when I first fell in love with the greyhounds. As I got older, I figured out that people don't always treat the greyhounds well. I remember seeing them get injured at the track and I felt so bad for them. I remember crying once when one of the dogs had to be taken from the track. I never forgot that and then when I was old enough to live on my own, I happened to meet some people who worked with dogs. Through them I met a couple who rescued greyhounds, and the rest is history. They were the reason I've had several rescues over the years. People don't realize it, but greyhounds make great pets. They're great with kids because they're so gentle and affectionate. The poor dogs who get injured on the track or are too old to race deserve happy lives."

Vanessa soon realized her connection to smoking and the greyhound breed had deep roots, especially with one of her favorite dogs:

SK: Where are you and when is this?

Vanessa: Egypt 1500 BC during the time of Amenhotep.[2]

SK: Very good. Are you a man or woman?

Vanessa: I am a boy. Very poor. I'm working and carrying stones from a quarry to help build a monument.

SK: How is this life affecting your current life?

Vanessa: I've always been a hard worker and I feel driven to work. I never let myself sit still for long. In those days, if you were caught resting for too long, you'd die either of the heat or by the hand of an angry boss.

SK: What about smoking?

Vanessa: Everybody does it. Nobody realizes it's not good for them and nobody cares. People don't live long enough to worry. Smoking is pleasurable, so why not?

---

2. New World Encyclopedia Contributors, *Amenhotep I*. 10 March 2016. 18:56. https://www.newworldencyclopedia.org/entry/Amenhotep_I.

SK: So you smoke too? Even as a boy?

Vanessa: Yes. I drink alcohol too. It helps with sore muscles and nobody cares.

SK: Is this the source event where your soul first smoked?

Vanessa: Yes.

SK: As you take a look around the area where you're working, is there anyone from that life you know in your current life?

Vanessa: (After a minute) There is someone there, yes. I see a super thin dog and when it approaches me, I try to offer it some food. That's my dog Elle who passed a few years ago. I have a new dog now, but Elle, she was something special. That's funny. I always felt like she was a very old friend. Now I know for sure I was right.

SK: What lessons did you and Elle learn?

Vanessa: It's about more than just her. She was my first experience with a greyhound and she's part of the reason I chose to be involved with them in my current life. She was a joy then during a very dismal period and she brought much joy to me in this life also, along with all the other greyhounds I've been around. They're truly ancient dogs and they deserve our help to continue on into the future. All animals matter, but the greyhounds are really special because they're such an integral part of ancient history. I've seen how graceful they are and what loving companions they can be. I have to do my part to ensure they continue to exist and thrive. Not that they'd go extinct or anything, but you never know. I want to help them. I see now this is part of my soul purpose.

The passion for animals certainly hadn't waned at all for Vanessa over the centuries. Last I heard from her, she had managed to cut down but still smoked on occasion.

Interesting to note, I did some research about her account of smoking in ancient Egypt. Tobacco was considered a product of the Americas that would not be available to ancient Egyptians. Or was it? Recent evidence suggests that Ramses II had tobacco fragments in his stomach, and that Egyptians may have crossed the seas to procure that and other treasures from the New World.[3]

I did not clarify whether or not Vanessa was actually talking about tobacco either. Smoking herbs and other rituals have been part of sacred traditions for eons. The physical act of smoking, rather than the nicotine and tobacco itself, could have left a psychic or holographic impression that compelled her to want to continue smoking in her current life.

As for her quitting, Vanessa's health scare turned out okay, so she hadn't reached the pain threshold sometimes required to make a lasting change.

Unfortunately, people are often motivated by pain. Sad but true. We don't take the class or seek guidance unless things are super challenging. I am happy Vanessa cut down, but I would have been more pleased to hear she had quit completely. That said, we are all on a journey and smoking is still a part of hers. Vanessa seemed to gain a further clarity about her life in other areas regarding purpose and a deep gratitude for her family ties that brought her tremendous healing benefits, even though she did not get the exact outcome she'd hoped for. At times we all want some magic wand to take away certain habits or troubles, but in the end, it's all about choice. Reconnecting with a friend, especially a loved animal from her deep past, proved to be a true blessing in Vanessa's life.

When you have a loved one who won't stop an undesirable behavior, one way to view it is that it's not any of your business to know or even try to comprehend what that person's soul has come to learn. In Vanessa's case, she is still learning through smoking, and I wish her well.

---

3. April Holloway. "Dealing in the Past: How Did Ancient Egyptians Get Nicotine and Cocaine?" 2 December 2017, https://www.ancient-origins.net/history/dealing-past -how-did-ancient-egyptians-get-nicotine-and-cocaine-009223.

Heidi Recalled a Childhood Trauma Involving Her Dog

Heidi was a corporate employee who had a fairly stable life—good friends, a great job, and a strong support system. Still, she had feelings of angst regarding her parents, who were quite strict and highly critical of everything she did. They expected her to be absolutely perfect.

During a regression involving her karmic links to her father, she discovered she had definitely known her dad in a prior life when the two lived in Africa during prehistoric times. In her current life, her father had passed away years earlier, and while the two were not in a bitter feud by any means, they had a cold wall of indifference that had built up between them over the years prior to his death. Her unresolved grief came from not knowing what to do with her contradictory emotions. During her regression Heidi relayed the following:

Heidi: I see my dad. He's the leader and I am also his daughter there. He's very egocentric and controlling, but with good reason. He has a lot of power and ability to communicate with the spirit world through a clicking language. He has healing abilities and people from all around bring their sick and ill family members to see him because he is often the only person alive who can actually help.

SK: Any idea where you live?

Heidi: Africa.

SK: What area? What tribe?

Heidi: (Thinking a bit) I don't know.

SK: Are you near water?

Heidi: No. Inland.

SK: Very good. What is the conflict with your father?

Heidi: He wants me to excel at everything and he tries to teach me how to do the healing work, but I don't believe I have the ability he does. I am more of a farmer. I enjoy the herbs and cooking, spending time with the other women, but he wants me to leave them behind and forget about all of that and learn from him instead.

SK: Is that acceptable? Are there other women healers in the area at that time?

Heidi: There are, but still, I don't want this life unless I can deliver the kind of results he does. I enjoy my animals and spend much of my time alone when I'm not helping with the cooking, gathering food, and enjoying the land.

SK: Very good. Fast-forward to the next most significant event in that life and be there now. What happens next?

Heidi: My father is angry, and he's taken one of my dogs. Not like the kind of dogs we have currently. It's more like a hyena that I've managed to domesticate. He was my friend and would go hunting for food with me. My father took him and gave him to the leader of another tribe in exchange for something—food, I think—with no regard for the fact that I loved that dog and he belonged to me. My father acts like everything is his and his alone. I'm so angry (tearing up). I can't stand him and what he's done to me. I move on, but I never fully forgive him.

SK: Would you be willing to let that go and forgive him now?

Heidi: (Wiping her tears) I'll try.

SK: Imagine a healing light is moving over that situation and let me know when this feels better.

Heidi: (After a minute) Yes, it's better.

SK: As you experience the energy of everyone you knew in your life in Africa, is there anyone else you recognize from your current life, yes or no?

Heidi: Yes. I had a dog when I was a little kid and I see he was my dog back then also. We had to give the dog away when we moved. I was really upset.

I did some research into some of Heidi's information and discovered there are two ancient tribes that have a clicking language: the Sandawe and Hadza.[4] The Sandawe people live in the area of modern-day Tanzania, far from the ocean, so it's possible this is where she was talking about. Later in the book, we will return to the discussion of Heidi's regression after she discovered her dog wasn't the only pet her father took from her in her previous lifetime.

Joel Adopted His Past Life Shepherd

Joel suffered from a midlife crisis of sorts and came to me to discover his purpose so he could move forward and find more meaningful work. He spent years as a stockbroker and found the task tedious:

"My job is soul-sucking. I know I have abilities and a knack for helping people navigate markets, and normally I feel good about that, but lately, with the volatility out there, some of my clients have lost a lot of money, and I feel like I'm doing more harm than good. I don't want to be the reason people lose their life's savings. I have to find something else to do that I can be proud of that helps others."

We discussed Joel's hobbies and interests to see what areas might offer clues to a better career option and he mentioned volunteering at a local animal shelter where he helped run the dogs. During his time as a volunteer, he wound up adopting a shepherd mix. During the regression, that information led to other clues about Joel's deep passion for animals:

---

4. Daniel Shriner, Fasil Tekola-Ayele, Adebowale Adeyemo, and Charles N. Rotimi. "Genetic Ancestry of Hadza and Sandawe Peoples Reveals Ancient Population Structure in Africa," *Genome Biology and Evolution*, Volume 10, Issue 3, March 2018, pages 875–882, https://doi.org/10.1093/gbe/evy051.

SK: What year is it and where are you?

Joel: Twenty thousand years ago. It's freezing and I am in a very cold, northern part of the world.

SK: What are you doing there?

Joel: Hunting to survive, catching whatever I can get my hands on.

SK: Are you alone or with other people?

Joel: Alone except for a big dog who comes with me. He and I have an understanding and we help each other and share food. Incredibly, when I look into his eyes, I see he's Duke, the dog I have now. We're still working as partners to this day.

SK: What lessons did you and Duke learn there?

Joel: It's better to work together for a common good than compete and try to take from others. There's enough to go around for everybody if we will share.

SK: How does this apply to your current situation with wanting to do something new with your life?

Joel: I've thought about buying a new building for our local shelter. I've been toying with it for years now. My wife says she's okay with it, but I've been dragging my feet. I've been extremely fortunate and I need to do more. This early partnership with my dog reminds me that these arrangements come back to you down the road. I owe it to him to do more than I am doing.

SK: Is this what you want to do with your life? Would that make you happy?

Joel: Yes. I don't need the money, per se. It's not like I'm going to disband my business altogether. I'll let my daughter-in-law run the place, which she pretty much does now. I'll go fund the building and I know there'll be a place for me on the board where I can make an impact. What good is the money if you can't use it to help people?

True to his word, Joel did help to fund the local shelter, and last I heard, he's still making a big impact on his community and enjoying time with family and his loyal friend, Duke.

Summing Up

The connection my clients had to man's best friend were so powerful, they spanned hundreds and even thousands of years. The old saying "love never dies" has never seemed so true.

Interesting to note that many of my male clients saw their dogs as partners in life, while the women had more emotional bonds with their dogs. Either way, dogs enriched the lives of people as they've done for thousands and thousands of years.

Chapter Three

PAST LIVES WITH HORSES, BIRDS, AND OTHER ANIMALS

THE DOMESTICATED HORSE HAS played an important role in daily life since the dawn of civilization and is understandably quite prominent in recollections of past life memories. Horses are an important part of the expansion of civilization because few other creatures offer both transportation and friendship to the humans they serve. The case studies definitely bring a greater appreciation for these majestic animals and cause us to take a moment of deep appreciation to honor all they've done through the ages to serve mankind.

In my current lifetime, my experience with horses has been limited to a couple of beginners' trail rides back in the days when I was a Girl Scout, and a few other times when I've ridden horses in large groups. Once in a while, I noticed a horse I was riding would gallop a bit and jerk forward and I would have a keen sense of fear rising up from within. During a past life regression, I accidentally uncovered the fact that I had indeed been thrown from a horse in Medieval England during a jousting tournament, and while the fall didn't kill me, the sword of my opponent did. My fall left me vulnerable to attack, and those feelings carried over into the mildest encounters with horses in my current life.

Although I am not at all afraid of horses, when I visit stables and I'm near horses, I feel a deep sense of respect and trepidation regarding the tremendous strength and power of horses in general. They are not at all to be trifled with. In one of my regressions, I recalled being kicked on several occasions in prior lives; one injury permanently damaged my intestines and left me vulnerable to injury, which was expressed during my current lifetime through the case of stage-four endometriosis mentioned earlier in the book.

Thoughts are things and everything that happens to us in past lives forms holographic memories that are stored within the body. The energetic pattern from my past life injury and current life illness has now been healed with a combination of past life regression and energy work, and I am pleased to say I no longer feel leery around horses.

In fact, once those situations were remedied, I had a powerful vision of a horse during a trip to China several years ago. One night I had a dream about a wooden horse galloping across the misty interior of my mind. Two days later while shopping in a gift store in my hotel in Shanghai, I saw the exact horse from my dream, which was sitting on the top shelf in the back corner. I took it out, held it in my hand, and checked for a price. When I showed it to the store owner, she told me that horse was not for sale under any circumstances. "Very old," she said.

"I have to have this," I explained. "I know this sounds crazy, but I had a dream about this exact horse a couple of nights ago."

When I told her this, her eyes grew wide and she stared at me.

"What's wrong? What does the horse mean?" I asked.

"Success," she answered, then took the little object over to the register and rang it up. "This is meant for you."

Horses are powerful symbols for success in China and other cultures. Horse images or statues put on the south wall bring fortune, according to Feng Shui followers.

Thanks to the fact horses are among the oldest of domesticated animals and have helped in tremendous ways with the development of humankind and the forging of civilization, there is no shortage of past life memories involving horses. No better companion has ever existed to provide strength, comfort, friendship, and protection to owners in all cultures around the world. We will explore past lives with horses in this chapter, as well as friendships that formed between people and other amazing birds and animals that changed people's lives both now and in the past. Enjoy!

Mina Asked for Help with Her Paint Horse

Despite my initial fear of horses, I've had considerable experience working with them because much of my work involves energy healing, combined with the fact that I've lived in Texas for the greater part of my life. My typical clients are human, but back in the day, I received several calls from frustrated pet owners who were at their wit's end. The clients had various problems with their animals and decided to give energy healing a try. I mainly worked with cats and smaller dogs, although horse owners also called quite often since horses are such sensitive creatures. When horses are troubled, those raw emotions can sometimes spook the horse, causing it to fall. When that happens, the outcome is often dire, so before the owners let the animal get to such a stressful state, when all else failed, they would try alternatives like energy healing.

Owners would call me out to the stables to help troubled horses calm down. All animals are sensitive to energy, of course, but horses respond exceptionally well to positive thoughts and vibrations. Likewise, if there is turmoil in the owner's life, such stress easily passes on to the horse during owner interactions during feedings and rides.

Mina owned a retail shop in a strip mall and kept her horses as a hobby. I knew her for years, long before I ever began my career as a healer, because I used to sell advertising in the local paper and she was a customer. Once I started doing my healing work, I felt comfortable letting her know what I did for a living. To my surprise, she was fairly open to alternative healing and told me all about her horses, and the fact that she was incredibly worried about her favorite gelding, Thor.

"Thor's upset about something. I don't think he likes his barn," she explained. "I've tried giving him the hay he likes, taking him on extra rides, brushing him more. Nothing's working." She stared at me a moment with an inquisitive look on her face. "Hmm, I wonder."

"What?" I asked.

"I'm going to have you go out there and look at him. Do whatever it is you do and see if you get anything."

At the time, I had never ever worked on a horse, but she insisted I try, so I went out to the stable with her one afternoon. Mina thought it might be better if she introduced us and then walk away, so she went back to her pickup truck and I stood on the outside of Thor's stall and watched him quietly for a while. After a few minutes, my hands warmed up and I began sending him some energy.

Working with such perceptive animals, you have to be aware that too much energy can sometimes do more harm than good and cause them to back away from you. So I gently sent the energy and attempted to clear my mind for whatever he wanted to tell me. To my amazement, Thor actually had a few things to say. When I returned to Mina's truck to give her the report about Thor's complaints, we determined, based on what I'd found, that she would greatly benefit from a past life regression.

Mina's horse "told" me she was right: He hated his new stall. He wanted to be with his friend, another horse that had passed away the month prior. Since Mina forgot to share that detail with me, she was stunned when I brought that up. "I forgot all about that part," she admitted.

"Animals grieve, too, you know?" I said. I also recommended she place an amethyst cluster and several big chunks of rose quartz in the stall to help him heal, which she did. "That's not all. He also says he's come here to be with you. You've known each other before." We did the regression to find out more details about their past life together, and Mina was beyond surprised by the information she received:

SK: Where are you and what year is this?

Mina: 1865, Alabama. It's the Civil War. I'm a soldier and I see Thor. He's my horse then also and he's got similar coloring and markings now to what he looked like back then.

SK: Very good. Fast-forward to the most significant event in that life as it relates to you and Thor, be there now, notice what's happening.

Mina: There's gunfire all around me. Smoke everywhere. Bullets flying. Very frightening. I hear him wince and realize he's been hit by a bullet. We're falling.

SK: Imagine a healing light comes down from above, surrounding you both, taking away any pain. What happened next?

Mina: We fall, but he's not dead. He blocked my body from other gunfire and wound up taking several bullets. Basically, he saved my life. I manage to get away with a broken arm, but I live thanks to him.

SK: How did your life in the Civil War relate to what you're doing together this time around and what are the two of you learning together as souls?

Mina: He saved me then and …(in tears) he saved me now. Not physically, but during my divorce, I rode him every day. If it wasn't for his company, I don't know what I would've done. I think he misses me and wants me to spend more time with him. I know I should be there more for him, especially now that my other horse has passed. I know better. I've just been so busy at the shop, but I promise I'll do better by him from now on. I owe him that much.

After placing the stones in the animal stable, Mina honored her commitment to shut her shop early on Wednesday afternoons so she could head to the stable and ride Thor one extra time per week on a regular basis. Time permitting, she also occasionally began visiting Thor whenever she could squeeze in an extra ride.

The transformation in Thor's attitude and overall health was instant and tangible. "He's back to his old self again, thanks to you," she told me.

"No," I said, "It's all you. He needed more love and you gave him what he wanted all along."

Our animals need us as much as we need them and, as Mina discovered, sometimes those feelings are carried over from the deep past.

Donna Tried to Save Her Horse from a Past Life Shooting

Donna asked me to come to her barn and do energy healing on her favorite horse, Dusty, who suddenly became lethargic for no apparent reason and had continued to go downhill for a week. When I asked Donna if anything traumatic had happened in her personal life, she explained that her only son had just gone off to college.

"My son left last week," she explained. "He's my only child, so I worry. I guess you'd say I'm overprotective. I don't mean to be, but I can't help it. Dusty belongs to both of us since my husband is out of town so much and doesn't ride. Sean normally rides him more than I do. Come to think of it, a few days before Sean left for school Dusty started acting up."

Once I worked on Dusty for a while by sending him energy, he noticeably began to calm down. Donna explained more about her struggles with her son's departure and decided to have a regression to try to overcome her protective nature. Donna found out that she and Dusty had a bond that went back further than she thought:

SK: What year is this, the first thing that comes to your mind?

Donna: 1698.

SK: Very good. Where are you?

Donna: (Thinking) Up in the northern part of North America. I'm a Sioux.

SK: Very good. Are you a man or a woman?

Donna: Woman.

SK: As you explore the energy of your life in the 1400s, is there anyone who looks or feels familiar to you?

Donna: (Crying) There he is.

SK: Who?

Donna: Dusty. He's my best friend there, just like he is now. He's the only person who understands me.

I am always surprised that I am not the only one who thinks of animals as people.

SK: Explain. What do you mean by that?

Donna: My … mate … he's always leaving me, going out for the hunt. I stay behind. My horse is my companion who saves me from being alone all the time. I'm not alone. I have a baby but he's too little to be much company. There are others in my tribe, too, of course, but they have their families and many of those men stay in camp more than my mate.

SK: As you experience the energy of the other tribe members, and in particular your mate, is there anyone there who looks or feels like someone you know from your current life?

Donna: (After a moment) Oh … yes … It's them.

SK: Who?

Donna: My husband and Sean. Sean is my baby and my husband is my mate. Things haven't changed much, I see. We used to live up in Wisconsin not too far from where we were then. My husband's never been around much in this life. Left me to raise Sean pretty much on my own while he was out on business trips, and here he is, riding away, and leaving me behind. He's a good provider then and now and I appreciate that, but he is missed. And now Sean's leaving. I feel alone like I did before.

SK: Fast-forward to the most significant event in that life. Be there now.

Donna: Oh! Oh no!

SK: What's happening?

Donna: (Crying) He killed him!

SK: Killed who?

Donna: (Still crying) My mate killed my horse and rode off so I wouldn't be able to leave. I run over to my poor horse. He's on the ground and I'm trying to save him, trying to stop the bleeding, but…(crying)… he's not going to make it.

SK: Imagine a healing light moves over those events, healing and transforming all of your pain. Let me know when it feels better.

Donna: (After a while) Yes. Better.

SK: Surrounded by light, fast-forward to the next most significant event in that life. Be there now. Notice what's happening.

Donna: I decide there and then to go on my own. My mate rode away. I pack up and leave.

SK: Were you able to survive?

Donna: Oh yes, quite well, actually.

SK: Very good. What lessons did the two of you learn together that you're still working on in your current life?

Donna: He's never liked the fact that I ride horses. In some ways, we don't have much in common other than Sean. I don't know what will happen now that he's gone off to school.

SK: How will your strength from that prior lifetime help you in your current situation?

Donna: My life is so good now compared to then. I have a nice home and maybe my husband and I can learn to do things together now that Sean isn't around. It's worth a try. Even though Sean isn't there, I'll survive, and everything will work out. One foot forward, one step at a time. Dusty will be a big help. I'd already planned to do some more riding. I know that will make Dusty happy and I'll enjoy it too. I can ask some of my friends to ride with me. Over time, things will get easier.

SK: What lessons are you learning from your horse Dusty in these lifetimes?

Donna: Dusty and I trust each other. We love each other no matter what. He's a great friend.

Once Donna did her personal healing and her regression helped her make an internal shift regarding her connection with Dusty, his strange behavior lessened. Donna accepted her new reality with her son gone, and the situation improved. I didn't hear from her after our session, so I assume Dusty did just fine after that. I certainly hope so.

Ralph's Gambling Began in an Arena in Istanbul

Ralph had a passion for gambling and nearly lost his marriage over his love of risk:

"I've been betting on horses since I was old enough to speak," he told me. "My dad got me into it, and his dad before him. When I did well in my business, I went out and bought my daughter a horse with the winnings, much to her mother's dismay, and I've been apologizing for that ever since. The horse was a rescue and needed a home. The second I looked into his eyes, I had to have him. Eventually my wife got over it and I found help and got over my gambling, for the most part, but no matter what I do, I'm still obsessed with the derby and any horse events on television. I don't take action on that. I don't go out and blow money on the betting anymore, but I think about gambling. Not on anything but horses though. Nobody can understand why. I grew up in Jersey and we never had horses other than what I saw on TV."

Ralph soon realized his love for the sport came from an ancient part of his soul:

SK: Where are you? What year is this?

Ralph: I'm in a huge stadium. I want to say Istanbul, Constantinople. This is early. Like 200s.

SK: What's happening there?

Ralph: I'm in a carriage racing around a track, fighting and clawing my way to try to win.

SK: Do you win?

Ralph: Sometimes, not always. You gotta try though, cause if you lose, there's a chance you'll be killed. I don't lose often.

SK: How did you get into this life as a racer?

Ralph: Not by choice. I am more of an indentured servant of some kind. I have to do this or I will be put to death. Race or die. That's it. If they don't like what I'm doing, I'm finished. Still, I come to love the sport. It's better than the alternative, that's for sure.

SK: Do you recognize anyone from that life in your current life?

Ralph: (Laughing) There's Chester, my daughter's horse! He's one of the horses back then. Poor fella. Those were rough times for all of us, but especially for the horses. They were definitely expendable.

SK: What lessons are the two of you learning?

Ralph: I had a soft spot for the animals back then. I hated to see them get hurt. We were equals, ya know? Same thing this time. When I saw him I had to help him out and he's been great for my daughter. She had some learning disabilities, nothing major, but caring for Chester helped her come out of her shell, so even though we helped him, I feel like we got the better end of the bargain. He's a great animal.

SK: Now that you understand the source of your horse fascination, will this help you with your urge to gamble?

Ralph: I've done a lot of therapy to get over that, but yeah, in a way this gives me more of a foundation I can draw on. I never thought about this before, but I think it's the suffering of the animals and the abuse that drives me to watch as much as anything. I hate seeing any animal mistreated even before I did this past life stuff, and I don't want anyone to suffer like we did to put on the show. That stuff still happens today. Hasn't changed too much, but it's still a rush to see them run.

Coming to higher understanding about the activities that cause addiction is another of the many gifts of past life regression. Ralph finally understood that his deeper purpose for loving the horses had a heart-centered meaning and wasn't simply a mindless obsession. From that vantage point, combined with the desire to help other living creatures, Ralph saw firsthand that great healing can occur.

Frank Rescued His Horse in a Past Life

Frank was a woodworker and craftsman—activities he did as hobbies. Like many of my clients, he worked in a grinding corporate job and hoped to find a better and more meaningful way to make a living. Frank lived on a ranch with his wife and kids and they had a couple of horses and chickens they kept for their personal use only. During an exploratory past life regression to deepen his understanding of his past life gifts and talents, Frank discovered an important and unexpected connection to his pet horse:

SK: Where are you and what year is this?

Frank: Southern Egypt, 2000 BC.

SK: What's happening?

Frank: I live in Luxor near the Karnak Temple. I only know that because I spend a lot of time watching shows about this place on Discovery Channel.

SK: Good job. What are you doing in southern Egypt in 2000 BC?

Frank: I'm a woodworker. I build furniture for the pharaoh and rulers.

SK: How did you learn your art?

Frank: An older man in our village showed me; he took me under his wing and taught the craft to me before he passed.

SK: How old are you there?

Frank: I'm a young boy. Maybe ten or eleven. I am really good at the work. The leaders make me work around the clock to build things, and eventually I begin building some of the items that will be put in the tombs.

SK: As you take a look around, is there anyone you know from your current life?

Frank: People, no, but I do see one of the horses from our ranch, a gelding named Apollo. He's there. In that life, I had to use dead horses for adhesives to hold my furniture together. In fact, I was one of the earlier people to find out how this works.

    When the building projects become more demanding, I overhear that they are planning to kill the horses and other animals to use for glues and adhesives. I sneak out in the night and release several of them from their pens. They run away to freedom.

SK: What happened to you as a result of doing this?

Frank: Nobody knows it was me. If they find out, I will be executed for sure. I continue to be successful, but I also insist we only use animals that have already died. For the most part that is easy enough to do because life is hard and people and animals don't live long. I feel like I was rewarded with a fairly prosperous and long life because I helped where I could and I did end up releasing other animals when I could so they wouldn't be needlessly harmed.

SK: Are there other lives where you've known your horse?

Frank: Yes, later in Persia. I raced him then. I hate to say I wasn't kind. I only valued money and power and in that life, I had both, but I became incredibly greedy. I suffered from a terrible back injury from a fall. My horse threw me because I mistreated him.

SK: Any other lifetimes?

Frank: Eastern Europe. I lived in a village and he was my work horse. I treated him kindly then, though, and he was faithful companion and friend.

SK: Any others?

Frank: No.

SK: What lessons did you and Apollo come together as souls to learn over many lifetimes?

Frank: Life is give-and-take. You get what you give. When I was kind, I received kindness. When I was cruel, I got what I deserved.

SK: How do these lives relate to what you should be doing now for work?

Frank: My own personal animals are enough. My artwork is something I should pursue more. I can see that I do have a genuine talent for woodworking and maybe I could make a business go. I've hesitated to do that, though, because I enjoy it so much. I don't want it to become a chore or something I have to do like I did in the past.

In my life in Egypt, if I didn't build what they wanted in time, I risked being killed. I never want that feeling again. When I think about my life in contrast to how things were then, I realize my current job isn't all that bad. Sure, there are talents we have and things we may enjoy more, but using those talents as a hobby is better.

Frank had a wonderful opportunity to explore his karma during the regression and last I heard, he hadn't made any changes to his career but instead used the regression to continue feeling gratitude for his life.

Mandy Recalled a Horse from a Spanish Ship Voyage

Mandy moved around her whole life and, as a result, her friends thought of her as the consummate free spirit.

"We didn't have much money when I was growing up. I was the oldest of five kids and my parents did the best they could, working odd jobs and moving around from town to town where they could find the most work in the farming industry. I've always sensed a deep love of the land and I wonder where that comes from. I've had dreams of being out on the plains in the past, like a pioneer. I wonder if that's something I saw on TV, or if it's real."

Earlier in the book, I mentioned that one of the primary arguments for skeptics of reincarnation is that people with memories simply regurgitate things they read or picked up somewhere else. That could have been the case with Mandy too. Unfortunately, I have no way to know with 100 percent certainty whether or not Mandy recalled an old TV show, or if her memories actually stemmed from her experiences in past lives.

When Mandy mentioned her doubts to me, she could either have been acknowledging the fact that on some deep subconscious level, she knew she saw this information elsewhere, or she may have been attempting to protect herself from feeling foolish. Most people who undergo regression experience a feeling that the things they're experiencing are not real, and they often describe them as sounding silly. Clients often tell me things like, "I feel like I'm making this up," or "I know this sounds nuts," or "I promise I'm not crazy." Part of the reason this happens is that the thoughts seem so random. I know from my own experiences the images, thoughts, and feelings appear out of nowhere and don't seem to be anything from my own personal memories. They're so out of thin air at times, it's natural for clients to question where the ideas come from. As long as I can convince clients to avoid judgment and go with where they see the images take them, healing can occur. From a therapeutic perspective, the healing, transformation, and personal insight is all that matters. Mandy learned some important details about her soul's journey:

SK: What year is this and where are you?

Mandy: 1500s. I'm on a huge wooden ship crossing the ocean.

SK: Very good. Where did you come from?

Mandy: Spain.

SK: What's happening on the ship?

Mandy: The conditions are terrible. Very crowded, everything stinks. Some people are ill.

SK: Are you a man or a woman?

Mandy: A girl. Well, late teens, but in those days, I guess I was like a woman.

SK: Anyone you know with you on the journey?

Mandy: Yes. My family is there. My parents, and I see one of my siblings. We're coming to make a better life for ourselves. My father was promised opportunity.

SK: Very good. Imagine you arrive at your destination. What happens next?

Mandy: My father becomes ill before we get there. He doesn't make it. My mother and brother and I are alone. We get off at a remote area. I believe in North America somewhere. Now we're out on this sandy beach in the middle of nowhere. Food is scarce. I see the soldiers from our ship. They brought animals with them. Horses. I see a horse that I recognize from a farm we lived on during my current life. The horse theoretically belonged to the people we rented from, but I took care of her.

She's there in the 1500s. She's one of soldiers' horses. She gets loose and I'm hearing that her descendants are still roaming free in that area to this day. My parents moved us to Georgia during one of our adventures and we went and saw those wild horses. I've never felt as connected to any place as I did to that area. Now I know why.

SK: What happens to you and your family in that early life as Spanish explorers?

Mandy: My mother marries another soldier. He's harsh with us, strict, but he provides food and shelter, which is the only reason my mother married him. When we first got off the ship, life was horrible and we had to fight for everything. Finding food was hard, and we had to rely on others to help us with housing.

When I get old enough, I marry and get out. My life turns out fairly good considering the hardships we endured. My husband was one of those officers. Much older than me. We have a small but nice home and that horse, my horse that I took care of, belonged to him. I took care of her then and now, even though she never belonged to me either time, and I don't even know her name.

SK: What lessons did you learn in that life with your family?

Mandy: My father came back in this life to be with my mother. They really do love each other. He moved us around out of that same sense of wanting something better. In this current time he never found it either. The good news is it didn't kill him this time. He never could be content with what he had, though. He was always looking for more.

SK: What about the horse? What lessons did you learn from taking care of her?

Mandy: The horse gives me a feeling of freedom even though neither of these horses were really ever that free. They have free spirits and when I watch them gallop in the pastures, I have that sense in my soul of finding something inspiring in my life.

Mandy left the session with a new perspective on her free-spirited nature and how her behavior originated. We spend our whole lifetimes trying to get to know ourselves deeply and understand our motives for doing certain things. Regression offers an amazing shortcut to unearth some of our hidden motivations so we can find peace in our lives.

Owen's Troubled Teens Led Him to a Past Life Companion

My client Owen overcame unbelievable adversity to make something positive out of his life. A troubled teen, he went to a court-ordered program in the mountains where he had to care for livestock and find himself in nature.

"There were some rough times in my teens, for sure," he admitted. "I didn't want to be sent away that summer, but I had no choice. My parents shipped me off to a remote ranch in Utah. We had to rise every morning before dawn, feed the hogs, milk the cows, tend the chickens, and if we were on good behavior, we'd get to help out in the horse stables in the afternoons, brushing and grooming them. That's how I learned to be a farrier. I also learned to ride out there, and I've kept horses ever since."

After overcoming his childhood, Owen went on to work in oilfields and amassed his own fortune, eventually owning a large horse ranch in West Texas. He wanted to have a regression to discover lifetimes where he also worked with horses:

SK: What year is this and where are you?

Owen: I'm in the Midwest on a wagon train. Looking out and all around me, there are wild horses galloping free in the wind. I'm not sure the year but I'm a teenager, about the same age I was when I was sent away. I'm kind of rambunctious. My parents have to keep me busy to keep me in line.

SK: Anyone from that early time who you know in your current life?

Owen: My parents then were the couple who ran the boys ranch in Utah. Super nice folks, really care about the kids. They haven't changed much. They taught me then how to take care of animals, how to respect nature, and learn to live independently. I also gained my love of horses from them. I run across one of the wild horses out there when we set up camp. He takes a liking to me and follows our caravan, staying by my side. He's the same horse I met out in Utah. He's the sole reason I had to buy my ranch. I had to help horses. They were out on their own then, just like we were, and it was rough, really rough, for everybody.

SK: Was this the only life when you had horses?

Owen: Oh no. Not by a long shot. I see several others. Asia, Europe, even in Greece. We always had horses. I was a soldier in the Roman

Army. Horses were part of life. I'm grateful I woke up to them in my current life. Without horses, life is not as exciting.

Owen made the most out of his success, offering scholarships to other troubled kids to attend a ranch similar to the one that helped him, and he continues his commitment to horses and livestock to this day.

Next, we will take a look at some of the other incredible birds and animals that helped their human counterparts both now and in the past.

Tom Met His Falcon before on the Asian Steppes

One of the most amazing case histories I've done involved Tom, a man who rescued falcons and discovered he had a rich history with birds.

"I've been drawn to falcons my whole life thanks to my grandfather. He taught me everything I know about how to work with them, how to help them when they're in a bind. I've always known they were part of me and I wonder if I have any past lives where I worked with falcons."

Tom did a regression and discovered he had worked with birds, but not with the falcons:

SK: What year is this and where are you?

Tom: Mongolia. Long ago … not sure the date.

SK: Very good. What's happening in Mongolia?

Tom: I'm a Mongolian, and oh! There's my grandfather. He's with me. We work with the golden eagles and train them as hunters. They become part of us, part of our family. We know them as well as we know each other, maybe better.

SK: Fast-forward through your life and tell me some of the experiences you shared with your eagles.

Tom: We're training them to hunt, smell food, and lift off to go find things for us. There's Manford. He's one of my rescue falcons I just released into the wild awhile back.

SK: You mean one from your current life?

Tom: Yes. I knew him back then, but in those days, he was an eagle.

SK: What lessons are Manford, the golden eagles, and your falcons teaching you in many lifetimes?

Tom: Respect, partnership, stewardship. We should live in harmony with nature and realize animals have much to teach us. We have to stop disrespecting our co-inhabitants on earth and treat them like family. That way, everybody wins.

Tom continued his wonderful work in falcon rescue and travels around teaching to this day. He makes good points we can all benefit from—the partnership with animals is important and should be preserved. He admitted that he had been fascinated by the Kazakh people of Mongolia who have trained their falcons for centuries. He discovered them accidentally in childhood and that attraction evolved into his love for the falcons. The heart of a person and the kindness within the soul definitely carries on from lifetime to lifetime.

George's Grandmother Became a Cardinal

There are lots of stories told through the ages about spirits inhabiting the bodies of animals in order to help us in the material world. One of my favorites involved my client George, who lost his grandmother a couple months before our session. He shared a strange tale about a cardinal who showed up shortly after her death:

"Right after Grandma passed, we started seeing this bright red cardinal in the tree. It sat there for hours on end, staring at us, not moving. Then, pretty soon, the crazy bird kept flying straight into the upstairs window of Grandma's house, banging its head really hard on the window of her old bedroom. We all thought it was weird at first, but we never thought much of it until the cardinal kept right on going, banging and banging. I felt sorry for it and I tried to shoo it away, but it wouldn't leave. Several other family members tried, too, but it kept going. After a few days of trying to help, we started joking that the bird was Grandma and she wanted back in her house. This went on for about a month, then the cardinal went away and we haven't seen it since."

During his session, George had a chance to thank his grandmother and find out more:

SK: Imagine your grandmother is here now and you can say whatever you'd like. Do that now, and let me know when you're finished, and tell me about any important details you'd like to share.

George: I'm telling her how much we kids appreciated and loved her and how much we love her farm. She's telling me some things about daily care of the place, and I am assuring her I will take care of that. Also, I'm asking her about the cardinal. She says that was her. She managed to become the cardinal for a while.

SK: Why did she do that?

George: She says that was an accident. She was confused when she passed. She fell asleep and took a nap and passed away in her sleep, so when she woke up and became aware, she didn't know where she was or how to move on. She finally realized where she was and knew she had passed away after the family kept talking to her. My sister helped a lot. She kept on talking to that cardinal. She'd say stuff like, "Grandma, you've passed on. You can't stay here anymore. Go into the light."

SK: And this helped?

George: Yes, she says it really did. She's thanking me for that and she wants me to tell my sister.

During George's past life regression, he discovered he'd known his grandmother before and had helped her in an earlier lifetime also:

SK: What year is this and where are you?

George: Japan, long ago. 1200s?

SK: Very good. What's happening in Japan in the 1200s?

George: I am part of a large extended family. My grandmother is there. She's my aunt. She teaches us about the spirits in everything— the birds, the trees.

SK: How does this apply to what you're doing now?

George: Our religion believed in spirits in all things. My aunt taught me that. She had a difficult life. She's dying and I am there, helping her into the afterlife. She is showing me how she lifted out of her body and went into a tiny bird. She flew away and found peace. I was meant to be with her and help her both times. I'd moved away from the farm for years, but I showed back up recently, just in time to help her make her transition.

SK: What lessons did the two of you come to learn together in these lifetimes?

George: The soul is immortal, we go on from here. What we do on earth counts. We are important. All life is sacred.

When the session ended, George seemed quite peaceful about the results and learning more about his grandmother, as well as some of the other details he'd uncovered. It's quite possible George described Shinto, the traditional religion of Japan,[5] whose practitioners believe in the spiritual nature of all things. I've not run into him since, but I hope he continues to recognize the divinity in all things. I have a good feeling he succeeded.

---

5. Innovation Design Co., Ltd., *Understanding Shinto—Japan's Ancient Religion* (Japanology, May 10, 2018) http://japanology.org/2018/05/understanding-shinto-japans-ancient-religion/.

Heidi's Past Life Bunny Left Her Too Soon

Earlier in the chapter about dogs, Heidi discovered her father had taken her dog away from her when they had shared a past life in an African tribe. I attempted to help her bring healing light to the situation so she could resolve complicated unresolved grief she felt after her father's passing, but when I did, Heidi realized something else:

Heidi: In that same life after my dog vanished, I found a rabbit in a field and brought it home. I was afraid it would get killed. When my father found out, he took that also. I never did find out what happened to him. I also thought of him as a pet. My father says we must respect the animals, but we are not to pamper them. He says I need to be stronger. I am so upset.

SK: Bring the white light over that situation as well. Allow your father's Higher Self to appear and imagine he can apologize to you. On whatever level, he did the best he could. Let me know when this feels better.

Heidi: It's good to see him. He looks happier than I remember.

SK: Very good.

Heidi: Okay. It's better.

SK: Now tell me how this situation relates to the relationship the two of you had in your current life.

Heidi: He hasn't changed much since then. He's still controlling. In fact (crying), I remember something similar he did in this life.

SK: What?

Heidi: He took my rabbit. The rabbit was part of a science class in my junior high. My teacher couldn't keep him, so I took him home. I kept the bunny, Mr. Wiggles, in my room. I made him a nice little house and used a paper shredder to make a comfortable bed for him. I loved that little guy, and then...(crying) one day when

I came home from school, Mr. Wiggles was gone. I went to my room to feed him and with no explanation, he was just ... gone. It was horrible. When I asked my parents about it, my mom apologized, and my dad said the rabbit was a filthy disease-infested rodent and he had to go before we caught something from him. That wasn't true. I found out my dad took him to a pet store and sold him. It still breaks my heart to this day. I can't tell you how much.

SK: As you experience the energy of everyone you knew in your life in Africa, is there anyone else you recognize from your current life, yes or no?

Heidi: Yes, my bunny from my past life is Mr. Wiggles.

SK: Why did your dog and bunny return to you in your current life? What lessons are you learning?

Heidi: Love and friendship. It's sad that my dad didn't change so we could be together longer though. It's like we're just playing out the same thing, only thousands of years later. I wish things had been different. I can't go back and change things I had no control over, though, so somehow, I will need to forgive my dad so I can get on with my life. I see now that of all the things that happened during my life, I still resent my dad for this, and I need to let that go.

SK: Let's get your dad's Higher Self out here to talk to your Higher Self. Imagine this is his soul, the higher part of his consciousness and that he is here right now. Ask your dad what lessons the two of you came here to learn together and what exactly he meant by taking your pets away. Ask him to tell you why he did what he did.

Heidi: I can't believe this, but he says he's sorry. I never heard those words come out of his mouth, not even once when he was alive.

SK: Good job. What else?

Heidi: He says he did those things to protect me. In the life in Africa, the leader of the other tribe was an enemy and his son wanted to marry me. My father feared for my safety and the other chief was intrigued by how I trained my dog, so he offered to give him the dog if he left and never came back. The same tribe took my bunny as an offering. And with Mr. Wiggles, Dad saw something on the news. He's saying he really thought I'd catch something, like an actual disease, if I kept him, and he wanted me safe.

SK: Wonderful. Knowing this, would you be willing to let go of this and forgive him now?

Heidi: Yes.

Heidi did forgive her dad, and although he wasn't alive anymore to see it, the healing she received from her regression and the surprising ties to Mr. Wiggles the rabbit opened the door for all her relationships to be healthier in the future. Heidi continued to thrive in her work world and last I saw her, she was still doing well.

Tony's Ferret Was a Past Life Rat

Tony wanted a regression to find out if it might help his insomnia, and help him get clues about some strange dreams that had been bothering him. By default, he accidentally learned something about his current pet ferret while going over a challenging life from the 1800s:

SK: What year is this and where are you?

Tony: India in the 1800s, although I can't tell the exact date.

SK: Very good. What's happening there?

Tony: I am a devout Hindu and I live on the streets outside a temple. Very poor, but I believe all things occur for a reason, so I'm not unhappy about my status. The only problem is the city is infested with rats. They're making people sick. I know it, but we can't harm them. They're God's creatures and it's against our religion. They swarm me while I sleep, some of them bite me, and I'm exhausted at times. I go inside the temple, but they're inside also. I can't get away from them no matter what I do.

SK: Very good. What lessons are you learning there and how does this apply to your insomnia?

Tony: This is part of it, a leftover.

SK: Is this the source event of your insomnia you're experiencing in your current life?

Tony: I'd say so, but somehow this also has something to do with my job. I let everyone walk all over me. My job is not a religion though, so I need to start standing up for myself to get ahead and ... oh!

SK: What's happening now?

Tony: (Laughing) It's JoJo!

SK: Who?

Tony: JoJo, my ferret! He's there with me in India! He was one of the rats in the temple.

SK: Very nice. What lessons did the two of you learn there in India that you're experiencing in your current life, and why has he returned to you?

Tony: JoJo is sorry for being such a pest. He's a quiet little guy now, sleeps a lot. Super sweet. I wanted to provide for him, give him a proper home, which I was unable to do in India because I was homeless then myself. We have a bond of friendship and look out for each other.

SK: Can JoJo encourage you on your path to being more assertive?

Tony: I never thought of that, but yes, he will definitely remind me of the life we've lived before. I see he's someone I can talk to about work. In fact, I do that all the time, but normally I'm complaining and he's just listening to me. JoJo can be a helpful influence for me if I open my mind more to that way of thinking. We're big buddies and we go way back.

Last I saw Tony, he had switched jobs and seemed to be doing better. As for JoJo, he has lived a far cushier life this time around than back in the old days of homelessness, and the two continue their unusual bond of friendship.

Christy Saw a Dolphin She'd Known in Atlantis

For those who have read my other work, you know that many of my clients recall lifetimes in the lost civilization of Atlantis. Christy relayed a story about her recent vacation that became important to her past life session:

"My friends and I took a road trip to Tampa and somewhere along the way, we stopped at one of the beaches and saw a school of dolphins swimming along the shoreline. We jumped in the water and had a chance to swim with them. I didn't know if they would approach us or not once we started wading out a bit, but they were so gentle and friendly. They actually started swimming circles around us. I loved it! The dolphins were adorable, and one in particular seemed to follow me around. I've always wondered what that was all about."

Christy found out she'd known that dolphin before:

SK: What year is this and where are you?

Christy: Very early. I'm in Atlantis. I can see myself working in a city formed of crystals. We are telepathic and we're using the crystals to help raise the vibrations of the planet. The dolphins are there too. They're teaching us about sound. And I do see the same dolphin that I met on my trip. When I looked into his eyes, I knew I'd known him before and what I see is that same soul, eons ago.

SK: What lessons did the dolphin help you with in the past and how can you benefit from that now?

Christy: We're in another critical stage on earth. The dolphin wants to remind me to care for the earth before it's too late. Also to quiet my mind and listen.

SK: To what?

Christy: To nature, to my Higher Self, to God … all we need is already here. We just have to look hard enough.

SK: How will you apply this experience to your current lifetime?

Christy: I need to get more involved and not sit on the sidelines. I'm working on that now. I need to trust myself, honor my intuition and know my intuitive guidance is coming from a high place. Stop second guessing myself.

Christy wrote me some time later and said she'd become a volunteer for an environmental and recycling group and she seemed happy. Apparently, the tie to the dolphin paid off.

Seth Helped Tend the Bees

You may recall Seth the vet from the earlier chapter on cats. He realized that he knew his shop cat Felix from back in the day when he served as a ringmaster in a Russian circus. As a veterinarian, Seth knew from an early age he had a calling to serve animals, so it wasn't surprising to find that he had more than one lifetime involving nature. He didn't expect to uncover a Spirit Guide from the insect world:

SK: Where are you now?

Seth: I want to say Holland.

SK: What's happening?

Seth: I am in a thick canvas suit and I'm walking in a field.

SK: Where are you going? Go ahead and keep walking forward through time until you arrive at your destination.

Seth: I'm there, at a tree. There's a huge honeycomb and I am extracting the honey. Bees are everywhere, swarming around, but I'm not afraid. They don't hurt me. I take a look to make sure their home is in good order, protected from the elements, which it is since this particular tree is still in good shape. There were times in the past where I see myself relocating them, and still, they never sting me.

SK: Very good. What happens next?

Seth: I get the honey and return to the village. Everybody's grateful to me because they can't get near the bees at all. They say I have a gift. I don't think so. I don't know why the bees accept me, but they do.

SK: Imagine you can go to the very last day of your life and notice how it is you pass into spirit. Be there now, surrounded by a protective light.

Seth: I'm old. I have a family, a wife and kids, grandkids who are all surrounding me. I am happy I've lived a good life here.

SK: What happens to the bees after your death?

Seth: I took one of my grandchildren under my wing. A little girl. She's going to tend to the bees now. She also has a gift.

SK: As you experience the energy of your family there in Holland, is there anyone you know now in your current life? Yes or no?

Seth: The girl. She's one of my new vet assistants. She does a great job and has the spiritual calling for veterinarian work. She's in school now, but someday she will open up her own practice. I am here to support her and encourage her. The world can never have too many people who know and care about animals.

SK: What is your connection with the bees?

Seth: Strange, but they're my guides. Like a Spirit Guide.

SK: In what way?

Seth: They teach me to be careful; that nature is a delicate balance, and they show me how to cooperate with everyone and accept others. We all have our part to play.

SK: What connection do you have with bees in your current life? Or do you?

Seth: Actually I do. The wasps and bees are around at times, but they never come too close to me and people always comment on how calm I am around them. That's because I know from this past experience they won't hurt me.

Anyone with an animal totem can always look up those connections in books and gain insight into why an animal shows up in your life at any given time. Seth proved that each connection we have with any living creature is personal and may mean slightly different things to different people.

Dream interpretation is the same way. What one person sees as the meaning for his or her dream may not resonate at all with someone else. Such messages are personal and the connections we have to our totems have more to do with our soul purpose and mission than we might think.

Later in the book, you'll have a chance to meet your own Animal Spirit Guides and see what kinds of messages they have to share with you.

Sylvia Ate Her Pet Guinea Pig in a Past Life

Sylvia had recently returned from a trip to Peru when she came to see me. Like many clients, she had a strong feeling that she had been to Peru in ancient times, and had several dreams since returning. The phenomenon of *Supretrovie*, externally induced past life memories, surfaced for her in an especially strong way when she visited Machu Picchu, so she came to have a regression to find out the details.

At times, tears are a necessary step in the healing process and in regressions, crying helps remove stuck energy so clients can have greater healing. Still, the last thing I wanted was for Sylvia to burst into tears, but that's what happened when she regressed back to her past life in Peru. In that culture, going back to ancient times, the guinea pig is considered a traditional dish and is still part of the menu in restaurants today. Unfortunately, Sylvia wasn't at all pleased when she found out that one of her beloved pets was dinner in a past life:

SK: What's wrong? Where are you and what's happening?

Sylvia: Peru 2000 BC. I see my pet Ginger there. She's with other guinea pigs, only she's not the same exact version she is now. The people in our village collect them and I am a little girl. I've become super attached to her. She's become my pet. I go looking for her one day and realize my father killed her and is serving her for dinner. I'm crying. He said we cannot become too attached. I'm so angry, I won't eat for days. My father doesn't care. He keeps killing them.

SK: What lessons are you and Ginger learning and why did you come together for these experiences?

Sylvia: I'm paying her back for that, although she is not upset with me and she's saying she understands.

SK: As you experience yourself there in Peru with Ginger, what connections do those events have with your familiarity with Machu Picchu?

Sylvia: None. That wasn't the same lifetime.

SK: Imagine you can go to the lifetime when you felt most familiar with Machu Picchu. Be there now. What year is this?

Sylvia: Much later, 1500s. I am a Spanish explorer. We are in the Peruvian Andes, but we never do see Machu Picchu. I also see the Peruvians are eating the guinea pigs and I won't partake.

SK: Had you ever been to the Machu Picchu area in a past life?

Sylvia: No. I must have been familiar with the energy of the Andes. I think I explored closer to Cusco, but never in Machu Picchu.

SK: What lessons did you learn in your life in Peru?

Sylvia: Respect for culture, and that unusual creatures and life-forms of different areas should be maintained and treasured.

SK: How can you apply this to your current life?

Sylvia: For starters, I think I'll buy Ginger a bigger cage!

Sylvia left her regression beyond surprised. She expected her connection with Peru to be quite different from what she uncovered during hypnosis. Her experience validates the regression process. If she wanted to make something up, she would have relayed a story where she lived at Machu Picchu. Instead, her connection to the Andes Mountains and her pet seemed to come out of the blue, from the depths of her soul.

Her revelation of never seeing Machu Picchu could have been why her soul was called back to that area—to finally do what the Spaniards never did—find the sacred site. Anytime in life when you go into a situation with certain expectations, things don't always work out how you planned. Regressions are like that also. Clients expect one thing and discover something totally different. And as for her guinea pig, Sylvia left her session having found a renewed appreciation for her little pet and the bond that brought them together.

Summing Up

All animals are special, and clients find that it's impossible to live rich, full lives without them. At times, animals help keep us alive to survive the lessons and adventures we came here to experience.

I've been heartened by the depth of love clients show toward all sorts of animals and the sense of duty and responsibility they carry with them through the centuries. Without nature and our animal kingdom, our planet would be a dismal place. Thankfully, our pets light up our lives and our world and will continue to do so throughout the rest of our lives and future lives.

Chapter Four

UNUSUAL ANIMAL REGRESSIONS

THIS CHAPTER WILL GO into some of the more far-out ideas regarding our *Past Lives with Pets,* including those that showed up more than one time in a single life, and clients who recalled past lives as animals.

Coming Back—Animals Returning in the Current Life

The idea that animals could pass away and return to the same lifetime with the same owner is something I've considered possible for several years, although it's not something I told anyone about. I certainly didn't want people to think I'm any crazier than they already do, but I could never quite explain a pair of cats I had in childhood and why they seemed so similar to another pair I owned as an adult. The idea that they were the same souls had occurred to me in the quiet part of my mind for quite some time, and only in the past few years have I had detailed conversations with other people who believe the same thing happened to them with some of their favorite pets. If human souls return to be with the ones they love, it only makes sense that pets would do the same. The difference is in their shorter life spans, which makes the concept possible.

While putting this book together, someone mentioned the fiction books by author W. Bruce Cameron, author of *A Dog's Journey*, which was made into a film. I don't know why I'd never heard of Cameron's books before, but when I glanced at the premise—that a dog reincarnates several times to help out the same owner—I was obviously fascinated. I headed to the library and found the book and read it in an afternoon. Unable to put it down, I found myself bawling my head off with each version of the dog passing away. In fact, I don't think I've ever cried as hard or in as many places in any book I've ever read. I'm a total softie when it comes to losing a pet, and this book had plenty of that. There is no doubt why the story has struck such a chord with the public.

Stories from my clients and reading Cameron's work caused me to delve deeper into the mystery in my own life about the set of cats who came back to finish up family business.

When I was a child, one of my grade school teachers came to class and announced that her cat had had kittens. Shortly thereafter, my family adopted Sachet, a beautiful calico cat with brown and black spots and a perfectly formed teardrop shape under her chin. Sachet was a sharp genius, a killer/hunter with keen instincts; a cat's cat and a model for the species.

A year later, we adopted another stray we named Sammy, who became my best buddy ever. Sam was a lover, not a killer; a black Persian-mixed fuzzball that couldn't harm a fly. He allowed me to carry him around like a sack of potatoes and wear him like a stole around my shoulders. Cute as a button, but as far as cats go he was a bit of a disgrace. Sam couldn't fight his way out of a paper bag if his life depended on it.

Despite these conflicting personalities, Sachet and Sam got along fairly well when they were little because they were about the same age. Sachet assumed a motherly role and washed Sam and cared for him. She was the alpha cat in charge, though, and she made no apologies where that was concerned. Sam happily allowed her to dote on him and all was well until everything changed. Sachet had been catting around the neighborhood at night and killing the neighbor's carp, dragging the large, expensive fish out of the pond and bringing them home as gifts for my mortified family.

Soon thereafter Sachet was hit by a car while crossing the street and had a pin put in her leg. Once she recovered, she continued her carp killing, went out for her nightly hunt, and then vanished. She dragged her weak body onto our porch a month later and my parents rushed her to the vet, but she didn't make it. She'd been poisoned.

Heartbroken, we moved on. Sammy became our only cat until he was lost during a move several years later. Somehow while we were unpacking from a cross-country move, Sammy got out and vanished. We searched for months but never found him. That also crushed me. I'm sure everybody's had a beloved pet either die too soon or get lost. You hear about this on the news how sometimes pets are reconnected with their owners. Sadly, in Sammy's case, that never happened.

Eventually, I decided to adopt a tiny kitten, a grey-and-white tabby that fit in the palm of my hand. After trying out several names, I settled in on a true original—Miss Kitty. Kitty grew up to become a killer like Sachet. Sharp as a whip, Miss Kitty brought trophies home such as lizards, birds, mice, and the like, much to the family's dismay.

Soon after, I adopted a black-and-white long-haired tuxedo cat from a Humane Society event. I named her Goo. Like Sachet and Sam, Kitty took control and cared for Goo like a mother, cleaning her and tending to all her needs. They curled up together on the couch just like Sachet and Sam had years earlier. Life went on until Miss Kitty vanished and returned a month later with a horrific injury to her left back leg—the same leg that Sachet had damaged in the car accident. We took Kitty to the vet and her wound eventually healed. The vet concluded she'd either been attacked by a coyote or a hawk.

Through the years, I could not ever get the coincidences in their behavior out of my mind. I developed the idea that these two cats had come back to our family to replay things a bit. In the current life, Goo died at age twelve and Kitty managed to outlive her, reaching a ripe old age of twenty. In an exploratory session, I discovered the cats had soul contracts with our family and each other.

Next up, I will share stories of others who believe they, too, have had their little beloveds show up more than once in their current lifetimes, and through the animals, learned valuable lessons about the nature of true and unconditional love and devotion.

Sylvia's Guinea Pig Returned a Few Times

In the last chapter you met Sylvia, who was mortified to discover her father had served her family pet for dinner during her past life in Peru. Sylvia vowed to make amends and did so through several different lifetimes when she owned her beloved pet guinea pig. She was so committed to her promise, she even discovered that the same exact soul had been with her a few times in her current life:

"I've had guinea pigs ever since I was a kid and I can see Ginger is the same soul I had as a kid, then later in my teens, my twenties, and now. I am here to help her have a good life, or in this case, lives, and she is here to offer me that same loving support she did in the past in Peru. She's not a dog or cat, I get that, and some people may not understand why I love her so much, but she's my friend and she's been there for me. I owe her a lot."

> SK: Imagine you can go back in time to your childhood, to the very first time you met your guinea pig in this life. Be there now. Notice what's happening.

> Sylvia: I'm the oldest and I see my parents bringing him home to me after they were away for the weekend. He was a boy that time. White with brown spots so we called him Spot. Super cute little guy. He was a baby. I don't think he lived long. I remember my

mom crying one day and she told me he had passed, although I never did see that.

SK: Very good. Fast-forward to the next time you met your little friend in your current life. Be there now. Notice what happens.

Sylvia: It's junior high. I'm busy with my friends, but my parents bought another guinea pig for my little sister. The cage is in her room and they're trying to teach her responsibility. This time Ginger is a girl and my sister named her Daisy.

SK: Do you play with Daisy at all?

Sylvia: Yes, to some degree. I hold her and show my sister how to pet her and feed her. She's super cute and she lived a lot longer. I remember she passed when I was in my early twenties. My sister was crushed. We all were.

SK: Fast-forward to the next time you met Ginger in this life. Be there now. What happened next?

Sylvia: I bought a townhouse when I moved for my job and decided I didn't want to live alone. I've always loved guinea pigs because they're so easy, so I bought Martin, my black-and-white furball. He lived about six years and passed away just before I got married. I guess he helped me get through my single years and once that was over, his purpose was finished, so he left.

SK: Very good. And what about Ginger? When did you get her?

Sylvia: About a year after I got married. I had to convince my husband to let me have her, but once he agreed he ended up loving her as much as I do. She's really great, friendly, and cute. We let her out of her cage at night and she watches TV with us. My husband's even convinced she likes football!

SK: Imagine you can invite the Higher Selves of all these pets to be with you now in your mind. Thank them for the role they played in your life path. What lessons did your two souls come to learn together?

Sylvia: I am paying back for what was done in Peru, but also my guinea pigs all agreed to come help me get through certain chapters in my life. Each supported me in a way and I am still grateful. Poor Ginger is getting up there now, too, and I will be so sad when she goes, but at some point, I'll probably have another guinea pig and hopefully it'll be her.

Like friends, animals show up in our lives for a reason, season, or lifetime, and that's definitely what happened for Sylvia.

Claire Recalled Meeting Her Cat in Childhood

Years ago, I discovered I wasn't the only person who believes a cat returned to me more than once in my lifetime. When Claire and I met, she mentioned she'd known her elderly orange tabby, Antoinette, earlier in her life.

"When I was a kid we found an orange kitten and named her Maria," Claire explained. "She was so tiny, the cutest little thing you've ever seen. Even though she was an indoor kitten, once in a while, she would follow us outside and we would have to carry her back in, then one day, she vanished. I never knew what happened. My parents theorized that she climbed up under the car where we'd found her before, sitting near the warm engine, and probably got carried away when my parents went off to work. We didn't find any evidence of that, thank God, but we had a feeling that's what had happened. Broke our hearts.

Then a few years ago, I had this orange cat show up out of nowhere. The moment our eyes met, I knew it was Maria. She came back to see if we could get things right this time. I worried at first that she belonged to someone so I put up posters, called around, but when nobody came to get her and I didn't get any calls, she moved into my house and hasn't strayed outdoors, not even once, ever since."

Claire had a past life regression to learn more about her soul purpose and talents and during that session, we did some healing work around her cats:

SK: Imagine little Maria is there with you now, and invite Antoinette to join you also. Ask them now to reconfirm that they are one in the same.

Claire: Oh yes, definitely.

SK: What lessons are you learning together as souls?

Claire: Antoinette says she's learned the hard way that rules are in place for a reason. She came back to help me now because when things get tougher than they already are, I'm going to need a friend who listens. She listens and she says she's not going anywhere, at least not until I get through all of this.

Claire's mother had been diagnosed with Alzheimer's and the disease had progressed considerably in the few months prior to our session. She discovered they had also been together before and because she was an only child and her father had passed away years earlier, she would soon be responsible for making a terribly difficult decision—to move her to a facility.

SK: Speak to your mom's Higher Self. What is she telling you?

Claire: She says that I need to do what I need to do and she understands that I can't continue on much longer. (Crying) I hate this though. I never intended to have her go anywhere.

SK: Go back to a life where the two of you knew each other before that might best explain the reasons for her diagnosis and why you're dealing with this situation in your current life. Be there now, tell me what's happening. Where are you? What year is this?

Claire: Very early. I'm getting Asia. I am in a village. I am born a girl but nobody wants girls. They're going to kill me. My mother was also my mom back then. I make it into adulthood thanks to her. She hides me away and when people do finally see me, she pretends I'm a boy so nobody will get rid of me. She sneaks around, kind of like what I'm doing with her now. I've tried to hide her condition and pretend it doesn't exist for as long as I can. Even in this life in China, I eventually grow up and have to leave her and go out on my own in the world and try to make it alone in a place where nobody knows our family. They would have been punished if anyone found out that my mom deceived everyone. I hate it, but in a way, my mom is going to need to do the same. Of course, I'll always visit her, but at some point, she won't know who I am anymore.

SK: What lessons are you two learning over the course of these lifetimes?

Claire: The importance of family, caring for others, thinking of other people, and putting their needs ahead of your own.

About six months after our session, Claire contacted me to say she had finally placed her mom in a group home. She mentioned that although it was the most difficult thing she'd ever done, she realized it was for the best. All the while, her dear cat Antoinette stayed right by her side, loving and supporting her through one of her life's most difficult chapters.

Past Lives as Animals

More often than one might think, clients happen to regress into past lives where they existed as other life-forms. Usually this happens by accident and can be quite shocking for some to digest. This aspect of regression is always fascinating to me, especially because the lessons described are so poignant and relevant to the client's soul growth. Because so many have reported past lives as animals through the course of my time in this field, I wanted to know if I'd ever been an animal, so out of curiosity, I decided to find out.

Whenever I guide my clients, I ask them to do their best to remain open-minded and not judge the thoughts that come into their minds regarding where certain lives occurred or when they happened. That's easier said than done. When I went to find out about my past lives with animals, I took a journey that involves looking at yourself in a mirror. What I saw shocked me. I was a huge cat, a huge beige female puma with the black circular markings around the edges of her nose and mouth. I reported that I lived high in the Andes Mountains near the border of modern-day Columbia and Brazil, and that this lifetime occurred roughly ten thousand years ago. Is this true? Can I verify my experience beyond a shadow of a doubt? Of course not. None of the stories in this book can be verified to such a degree, but the point of doing them is to provide understanding about the inner workings of the soul.

In my journey, I saw myself climbing around the mountainous region as a female puma. I had a litter of four cubs, and while I was out hunting, a huge black boar, with tusks longer than those we see now, mortally wounded me. I experienced myself bleeding out and floating away, my only concern was the cubs and what would happen to them in my absence.

The puma is basically the same as a modern mountain lion and a close relative to the panther, a cat I've always been attracted to as a totem. Like many of my clients, even I can't say for sure whether or not any of this was real, other than the fact that the images certainly seemed real as day during the session. My regression felt helpful to me and provided me insight into my connection with cats as I came to understand that because of this bond from times long ago, I still maintain a close connection to all felines.

In this next section, I'll share incredible stories of clients who mostly discovered their animal roots accidentally but found greater understanding about themselves in the process. Later on, you'll have a chance to discover your own past lives in animal form. Enjoy!

Clyde's Past Life as a Dog Caused Back Issues

Clyde came to see me, as many people do, to attempt to find answers and get to the source of his nagging back issues.

"I've been to too many doctors to name, I've tried every medicine in the book and I've just finished my third surgery. Nothing's helping and I refuse to become a drug addict over this. There's got to be more to my issue. I'm willing to try anything at this point."

Clyde visited a past life where he'd been injured:

SK: What year is this and where are you?

Clyde: Roman times. I'm a soldier and I'm being stabbed to death in the back by a sword.

SK: Point to that area. Is this the same area of the body causing issues in your current life?

Clyde: (Pointing to lower back) Yes.

SK: Very good. Let's bring a healing light in now to wash over that wound, healing every single cell, transforming this injury. Bring out the soldier you were then and notice a cord of light between you. When I count to three, that cord will be cut and you will be released from this injury and its effects. Ready? One, two, three, cutting that cord. Allow a healing light to wash over you both, transforming this pain. Let me know when this feels better.

Clyde: (After a moment) Yes. It's better.

SK: Is this the source event of your back issue?

Clyde: No. There's another earlier injury causing problems also.

SK: Very good. Be there now, notice what's happening. Where are you?

Clyde: I want to say Africa? Pretty early on. Not sure when. Sounds strange, but 4000 BC comes to mind.

SK: What's happening in Africa?

Clyde: Not sure.

SK: Are you a man or woman?

Clyde: Neither?

SK: Imagine a mirror floats down. Look in the mirror, notice what you see.

Clyde: I can't believe I'm saying this, but I'm a dog of some kind. Not like what we have these days. I'm wild. A wandering animal. And I'm huge. I'm a lot like a wolf, only I have strange coloring and longer legs. Not like a hyena either. Something different.

SK: Very good. Notice what happens that causes your injuries and be there now.

Clyde: I'm injured in a fight with another dog. He's vicious and leaps from a bush on the Savanna and lands right on my lower back and cracks my spine. I die a slow and painful death.

SK: Bring a white light into that injury and event. What lessons did you learn in your life as a wild dog?

Clyde: Self-reliance. You may run in a pack, but they can turn on you and leave you to survive alone.

SK: How did that experience help you in your current life?

Clyde: My parents split when I was a baby and I had to do a lot on my own. I had to grow up fast in what I thought was a tough environment. Now I can see that the Savanna was a lot worse.

SK: Are you ready to let go of these injuries?

Clyde: Yes.

We did more healing on these two injuries and talking about the spiritual significance of the back, which often relates to feeling unsupported in life. The discussion about the wild dog brought up more opportunities for healing and forgiving where Clyde's parents were concerned—forgiving his father for leaving, and thanking and finding even more gratitude than he already had for his mother, who did the best she could under difficult circumstances. Clyde seemed more relaxed after his session and I hope his back improved, although unfortunately, I haven't heard from him.

Jim Recalled His Life as an English Pointer

My client Jim was an avid hunter when he came to see me after he and his wife took a trip to England that left him more than a little confused.

"My wife and I were traveling by train through England. We left London, headed for Edinburgh, Scotland, looked around, then came back toward London. While we were in the Wales area, we stopped in a tiny village to take a look around and all of the sudden the modern cars vanished and I felt like I'd entered a time warp from a long, long time ago. My wife said she felt like she'd been there before too. I thought I might have lost my mind."

Like some of the clients mentioned previously, Jim experienced *Supretrovie*, a spontaneously induced past life memory brought on by travel. Although he believed he might need mental health intervention, Jim's experience is quite common. Most people experience some form of

Supretrovie during their lives, which can be brought on by the location they're in, meeting a person they've known in a past life, or by coming into contact with various objects that they've either seen before or that remind them of things they've seen before.

When *Supretrovie* happens, clients need past life regression not to remember the past life but to heal from that memory. Jim soon regressed into a time in England:

SK: What year is this? The first thing that comes into your mind?

Jim: (Confused) I don't know.

SK: Where are you?

Jim: Hard to say, but it seems near where my wife and I visited on our trip.

SK: England?

Jim: Yes.

SK: Very good. What's happening in England? Be there now. Imagine you can easily notice.

Jim: (Hesitating) It's hard to say.

SK: Are you a man or a woman?

Jim: I don't know.

SK: Go ahead and look at your feet. Notice what kind of shoes you're wearing.

Jim: (Gasps)

SK: What's wrong?

Jim: I see paws, not feet.

SK: Very good. Go ahead now and imagine a giant mirror floats down in front of you. Be there now. Notice what you see in that mirror.

Jim: I'm looking at one of those hunting dogs like the ones they have in Britain. My wife and I saw several on our trip.

SK: What color? Describe the dog.

Jim: White mostly, with brown spots, freckles. Kind of like the freckles I have now. I'm one of those dogs. I know that sounds nuts.

SK: Very good. Go ahead and fast-forward into your life as this dog in England. Notice what's happening.

Jim: My vantage point is lower than I'm used to, but I see the men on horses. We're running through the woods pointing out animals. I do well. My master is pleased.

SK: As you experience the energy of other people and animals around you, is there anyone who looks or feels like someone you know from your current life?

Jim: My wife is definitely there somewhere. She is a lady who lives in that village, but I did not necessarily know her. (Pausing) Wait. I think she's my master's daughter.

SK: Very good. What lessons did you learn in that lifetime?

Jim: Loyalty, hard work, companionship.

SK: What about the lessons with your wife? What are the two of you learning together?

Jim: She was kind to me, kind to all animals. She's still that way now. A truly compassionate lady.

SK: What about you? Why did you choose to be a dog?

Jim: To experience different forms of life and understand one is not better than another. All life has value.

SK: How does your life in England affect you in your current lifetime?

Jim: My wife and I are still avid animal lovers. We have lots of dogs. In fact, my dad had a similar hunting dog when I was a kid. We'd take him out to help us drum up grouse and quail.

SK: Fast-forward to the very last day of that life you lived as a dog. Be there now. Notice how you pass into spirit and do that now.

Jim: I'm shot on a mission. My master is upset. He jumps off his horse and comes up and pets my head. He's telling me I'm a good boy. I'm in pain, but I'm happy and I go to sleep.

SK: Float into that peaceful space in between lives. What lessons besides loyalty and companionship did you learn as a dog?

Jim: Unconditional devotion, love, and how to enjoy the little things in life.

After our session, we did some internet searching to find out what exactly Jim had seen and discovered, based on his input, that he was a brown-and-white pointer. Jim contacted me some time later with an emailed photo of his new pointer puppy. He explained that throughout his life, he'd never used any of his dogs for hunting; a fact he now attributed to his former incarnation. His new puppy would also never see a day for hunting and he bought her for friendship only. His wife loved the dog as much as he did. Jim also said that ever since his regression he'd given up hunting altogether. "I now feel that hunting is dangerous for everyone and not worth the loss of life," he told me.

No doubt powerful past life memories can drastically alter our current life behavior. That's exactly what happened to Jim.

Lydia's Sensitivity Began during Her Life as an Aztec Chihuahua

Lydia decided to have a past life regression to hopefully explain and help alleviate her anxiety over her stressful job:

"My work is insane. I work in a huge call center with hundreds of people. I'm always nice, but when people call, they're rude and mean. Not everyone, but a lot of them. I'm not sure how much longer I can take it. I'm super thin-skinned and I shake when the customers shout at me. I know I'm too sensitive, but I don't know what to do about that. I can't help it. Besides, nobody deserves to be treated like that, no matter what.

"I've walked away from my desk a couple times and, of course, I got called into my boss's office to explain myself. Once I hung up on a woman who was so rude, I couldn't deal with her. That's against the rules, of course. We're not allowed to hang up or get upset at all on the phones. If I don't get myself under control, I won't have a job. What's more upsetting is that I'm worried about what this says about me as a person that I don't just get up and leave and go work at a place where people treat me right."

The session delved into current-life issues regarding Lydia's family. Her hypercritical mother had caused her to feel insecure in many ways, so we did a healing about that and then ventured into her past lives where she discovered a shocking revelation about herself:

SK: What year is this?

Lydia: 1300s? That's what I'm getting, although I can't say for sure.

SK: Very good. Where are you in the world?

Lydia: Mexico.

SK: Look around in Mexico in the 1300s and tell me what you see.

Lydia: Pyramids, people, all towering over me. I'm in a market crammed in a cage. I'm shaking and scared for my life.

Lydia's description of her circumstances sounded a bit off to me, so I asked for clarification:

SK: Are you a man or woman?

Lydia: I'm not sure.

SK: Imagine you can look down at your feet and notice what you're wearing.

Lydia: (Gasping) Oh my God! I see feet!

SK: What kind of feet?

Lydia: Brown furry feet.

SK: Imagine a mirror floats down in front of you. Look in that mirror, tell me what you see.

Lydia: I'm a tiny brown dog. Kind of like a Chihuahua, only not quite.

SK: What's happening that's frightening you?

Lydia: They're taking us away and I see them killing us for food!

Normally I guide clients into viewing their last day of life, but not in Lydia's case.

SK: Go ahead and lift up out of that body, out of that life. Float into the clouds in a peaceful space in between lives and imagine you can know how you passed away.

Lydia: They killed me and put me on the altar as a sacrifice to the gods. Now that I think of it, I did go to Mexico City once and visited those pyramids north of there and I couldn't take it. I threw up and got violently ill. Now I know why. I lived there before during the times of the Aztecs.

SK: How did your experience as a Chihuahua affect your current life?

Lydia: The nervousness, which happened for a reason, is part of who I am. I brought it in with me. That energy is nothing but pure fear.

SK: Do you have other lives where you also felt especially sensitive between then and now?

Lydia: Yes.

SK: Fast-forward to that life, be there now and notice what's happening. Where are you? What year is it?

Lydia: Somewhere in the desert in the Middle East. The year is 1600-something.

SK: Very good. What's happening?

Lydia: I am married to a very cruel man who berates me and shouts all the time. I am property, nothing more. He has lots of wives and treats most of us the same with the exception of his favorite.

SK: Fast-forward through the life and notice how you pass into spirit.

Lydia: He killed me. He didn't mean to, but he was angry. He hit me and I fell and hit my head.

SK: Move into the peaceful space in between lives. How does this life from the 1600s affect you now?

Lydia: I am still afraid when I hear anyone yelling. It's so bad that they don't actually need to be raising their voice. It's a tone I'm scared of. If anyone starts to get a tone that suggests they're unhappy, I immediately go into a panic.

We worked for some time doing healing around the Aztec situation, and later around the tone of voices. We also brought healing light to several other incidents in her current life where people's tones were perhaps misinterpreted. Lydia said she could see why her boss accused her of overreacting, although I assured her that based on all she described, her feelings were normal. I also mentioned that perhaps call center work would be better suited to someone with thicker skin and that she didn't personally need to change. The world needs sensitive people, and rather than changing her kind behavior, changing her working conditions could make her life better.

She wrote me about a year after our session and said she'd found a job in a quiet office where she had a few pleasant coworkers and did more solitary work where she was judged on accuracy. She dealt face-to-face with the public on occasion and found that most of the people who came in to the business were kind people. She found greater happiness by embracing who she was and accepting herself with all her good qualities, which we should all do. Self-improvement is admirable, but at times, the biggest improvement you can make is learning to appreciate the person who should matter most—yourself.

Sid's Connection to Canada Had Ties to the Bear

Clients often want to use their past life regression as a guide to help plan future events. By delving into past scenarios and consciously recalling what happened to our souls in past experiences, clients can make informed decisions to move forward in life. Sid wondered if he should continue to stay in Canada. He loved his home and enjoyed the rugged environment he'd grown accustomed to, but well-meaning family members suggested he might fare better in a large city with more job opportunities. The session gave Sid great clarity on his soul purpose and mission:

SK: Go back to a time that would best explain where you're supposed to be living now. Be there now. Where are you and what year is it?

Sid: 1600s in the Canadian Rockies. Not too far from where I live now.

SK: Are you a man or woman?

Sid: (Hesitating) I'm not sure.

SK: Glance down at your feet. Notice what you're wearing.

Sid: I have large paws. They're bear paws.

SK: Very good. What are you doing in the Canadian Rockies as a bear?

Sid: Fishing, walking the land…

SK: What lessons did you learn in your life as a bear and how does this relate to where you're supposed to be living?

Sid: Nature is the most important consideration for me. Being out in nature. Joy in life has nothing to do with material pursuits. I lived there then and I chose to come back into this area during my current life because this is a positive area and a good influence on my soul. I need to stop listening to what everybody else wants for me and stay here.

The soul will return to places where it lived before, to locations where the spirit had positive experiences or where growth can best happen. In Sid's case, he discovered that he was right where he was meant to be all along, only perhaps in not the form he expected. One of the amazing surprises on the path of self-discovery.

Andrea Had Little to Say about Her Life as a Horse

Andrea had a surprise when she discovered her past life as a horse, but when I tried to get more information from her about the life and the bigger meaning in her soul's purpose, she was incredibly short of vocabulary:

SK: Where are you and what's happening?

Andrea: Trees. I see trees and apples. Mmmmm, they taste so good!

SK: Fast-forward to the next most significant event. What happens next?

Andrea: Trees, the trees… and the apples.

With many of the cases of clients reverting to animal form, they are often confused and at a lack of words for what they're experiencing, although Andrea proved the most extreme case of this I've ever encountered. I kept rephrasing my questioning, waiting for responses that never came and trying to get more of a description of where she was in the world, what the year was and how this could be of benefit to her in her current life. All the while, she was unable to explain any of this to me. Finally, I realized Andrea had gone into such a deep state of hypnosis that she seemed to have temporarily lost her vocabulary.

In all my sessions, I use a particular process I've developed to quickly and easily allow clients to access the information that will help them in the best way possible without going into deep hypnosis. The process quiets the skeptical part of the mind while allowing free-flowing thought to come through. I've learned over the years it's better not to take people into super-deep trance states: first, because it's not necessary; and second, because in those deeper states, they're less likely to recall what happened. To me, the whole point of doing the journey is to remember what happened so you can return from your journey and use that powerful information to make positive changes in your current life. That said, despite my best efforts to keep the trances lighter, some clients are incredibly prone to suggestion and go far deeper into trance than the majority of my clients. You would see people like this if you ever try one of those stage-hypnosis shows. There are folks there who will go all in and act like clowns, stomping around the stage, doing whatever the hypnotist suggests. People ask me all the time if I think such displays are real or if the person is merely faking and hamming it up for showmanship purposes. Usually I do believe these subjects have been actually hypnotized—only deeper than most of us would be willing to go. In Andrea's case, she certainly had a full experience of her life as a horse. When she came to, I asked her if she remembered what she'd said, and to my surprise, she did.

"That life was so lovely. I want to hold that image of the grassy fields and the apples in my mind forever to remind me not to take life so seriously. The simple things are all that matter."

Andrea proved that you can re-emerge from a deep hypnotic state and still be impacted by the healing and learning you receive.

Ray Enjoyed a Quiet Life as a Farm Horse

Ray was one of the few clients who came in wanting to explore past lives in animal form. Typically, these epiphanies come up spontaneously, but with Ray, he seemed to have a case of what Carl Jung called anamnesis, a soul knowing who he was in the past:

"I've always believed I used to be a horse in a past life, even though I don't own any or live around them in my current life. I have a connection with horses I can't explain. I'd love to go back and see if I come up with anything on that because it's an idea I've been curious about for years."

Although I thought it might be possible that Ray owned horses or lived near them in the past, to my surprise, Ray did indeed access a memory from a few hundred years ago:

> *SK:* Go back in time to a life that would best explain your attraction to horses. Be there now, notice what's happening. Where are you? What year is this?
>
> *Ray:* I'm at a farm in South Carolina in 1803. I'm a horse and my owner is a deputy sheriff who takes great care of me. We had a bad drought and he makes sure to boil all our water, and that I have safe drinking water and food, even though food is hard to come by.
>
> *SK:* Fast-forward to the last day of your life in South Carolina. Be there now. Notice what's happening. What year is it?

Ray: It's 1823. I'm in my stable and I'm old. I accidentally tripped and broke my leg. My master is petting my head. He is saying goodbye. He sees I'm in horrible agony and he doesn't want me to suffer so he shoots me. I leave instantly and I don't feel any pain.

SK: Surrounded by loving light, float up and out of that body, into the peaceful space in between lives. Be there now and allow the light to move over your owner.

Ray: He's crying. He didn't want to have to do that.

SK: Very good. What lessons did you and your owner learn about together?

Ray: Love, friendship, companionship. All life is valuable.

SK: Was the sheriff anyone you know in your current life?

Ray: I think it's my older brother. He's been a real role model for me and in a way, he's had to take care of me a lot in this life also.

SK: What will you take out of your life as a horse that you can relate to in your current lifetime?

Ray: Simplicity. Taking things slowly. Appreciation for what you have and enjoying the outdoors.

Ray told me how happy he was to finally know about his past as a horse. He worked as an accountant and had a nice quiet life with a sweet family and lived in the same way as he had long ago as a horse—with simplicity and gratitude. We can all learn from his example.

Stephanie Recalled Her Life as a Tibetan Snow Leopard

Stephanie wanted a past life regression to uncover her attraction to Buddhism, Tibet, and Asia in general, even though she had never been there during her current lifetime and had been raised in a strict Christian home. During her lifetime, the belief systems she grew up with no longer resonated with her; she wondered why and assumed she lived a past life as a Buddhist. She wound up discovering her connection wasn't from any actual experiences as a Buddhist herself:

SK: Where are you? What year is this?

Stephanie: I want to say 1200s in Tibet. There's snow all around. It's super cold out, but I am not affected by the weather at all.

SK: Why not?

Stephanie: I am on all fours. I see my huge white paws and I am climbing a cliff. I am a leopard.

SK: So you're a leopard?

Stephanie: I know that sounds crazy, but yes.

SK: Describe your life and how this connects you with your attraction to that part of the world.

Stephanie: I roam in the mountains and I am aware of the monks in the monastery. They are kind men who leave me food when the winters are especially harsh. I can sense the vibrations from their music and chanting and I am attracted to that energy. I have a very innate sense of the holiness of that place and the positive intentions they put into our world.

SK: Imagine you can ask your angel if you've lived any other lifetimes in Tibet. Yes or no?

Stephanie: No.

SK: Have you been a Buddhist in any past lives?

Stephanie: No. I've lived in Asia in the past. I'm hearing in China once or twice, but I did not follow Buddhism. The reason I am so attracted to that teaching is from my experience as a large cat and the kindness of those people.

SK: What lessons did you learn in your life as a leopard?

Stephanie: Self-reliance combined with luck and charity of other kind souls can carry you through life.

Stephanie certainly had an interesting journey and her regression gave answers that were not at all what she expected. That happens quite often. In my next case study, I was the one who had the biggest surprise.

James Was a Shark in Business and in a Past Life

I am a huge believer in going with the flow when it comes to these sessions. I repeatedly tell people to use the power of the imagination to come up with healing rationale that makes sense to them, even if it theoretically doesn't make any sense at all to the "real world." I don't judge, because you never know what or why people come up with the stories they tell themselves during hypnosis.

James proved to be one of the more unusual subjects that made me wonder if he had actually experienced the lifetime he relayed to me, or if his memory was simply the byproduct of too much Shark Week programming on television. Nevertheless, he seemed to find self-understanding through his story, and the explanation of his deeper connections to sharks certainly intrigued me.

James had a high-powered career and traveled around the world on exotic, daring trips that most people wouldn't care to experience. During a tour of South Africa, he decided to entertain himself with a thrilling adventure:

"While everybody else was out at a winery, I hired a guide and had them take me off the coast in a high-speed boat where I was put into a cage and dunked into the ocean so I could see the sharks face-to-face. The water was frigid, but I loved it. What was weird and the reason why I'm here is because I felt so at home in the ocean there. Sure, I've taken scuba classes before, but there was something about that water that I loved. The sharks swarmed all around us and I noticed some of them butting heads with other people's cages, like they were trying to get in there and chomp them down, but with me, when any of them approached, they came real close, looked right in my eyes and they were calm. Why is that?"

James went into a prehistoric past life and came up with some pretty unbelievable answers:

SK: When is this and where are you?

James: At least a million years ago, maybe more.

SK: Where are you?

James: The ocean. I don't know where in the ocean, but I'm deep in very cold water.

SK: Great, how do you feel in the ocean?

James: I'm hungry. I'm swimming around trying to catch something. That's all I think about—food.

SK: Fast-forward to the moment you find food. If you do, be there now; notice what's happening.

James: Not too much longer, I'm gliding along and I see a school of fish. I open my mouth and suck them in. They don't even know what hit them.

SK: Imagine you can bring a mirror down from above and that mirror can float in the water in front of you. Look in that mirror now and tell me what you see.

James: (Chuckling) Oh my God! I knew it!

SK: What?

James: I'm a shark! No wonder those guys loved me in Africa!

SK: Very good. What lessons are you learning as a shark?

James: Sharks are a form of ancient consciousness. Being a shark taught me about survival of the fittest. There's always something that could get to you, but if you're aggressive and let people know who's boss, you can do what you want in life.

SK: How did your life as a shark relate to your current situation?

James: Business is like that. I built my business from the ground up. I always play fair, but I make sure people know who they're dealing with, and I don't play games. I get what I want.

James was quite a character, for sure, and he definitely proved that sharks in business do become successful. In terms of soul purpose, James enjoyed traveling, perhaps because he was such an old soul, he wanted to return to familiar places. Another possibility is his story could have merely been an archetypal experience of what we've come to define as sharklike characteristics. Either way, he was pleased with his session and believed it helped him understand himself better, so that's the most important aspect of any session.

Lenore Was a Lemurian Lemur

To end this section of the book on a far-out note, my client Lenore was one of many who believed in the ancient Lemurian civilization that pre-dated Atlantis. Through the years, I've had many clients relay stories about their past lives in these prehistoric times. Many clients recall lives where they existed solely as light, but Lenore's story differed when she claimed to be a reincarnated Lemur:

Lenore: I live in a very early time in Lemuria. Not at the very beginning, but after formed beings began inhabiting the planet.

SK: When?

Lenore: Millions of years ago.

SK: Where?

Lenore: I can't say. I live in a jungle and my life is very quiet and peaceful.

SK: Notice a mirror in front of you. What do you see?

Lenore: I am a Lemur—furry face, ringed tail. I crawl and climb in the trees and eat fruit.

SK: What lessons did you learn in your life as a Lemur?

Lenore: Being.

SK: Being?

Lenore: Yes. Being still, not having an agenda. Living for the sake of living and expressing joy and love toward all other living creatures, whether they're plants, animals, or insects.

SK: How is your life in Lemuria influencing you now?

Lenore: I try to be peaceful, although that's easier said than done sometimes. I used to have a stressful job, but as I've gotten older, I enjoy experiencing more silence and stillness. Now that I've remembered this past life, I hope I can bring that memory into more of my daily experience. Also, we need to love each other. That's the only reason we're alive. To love.

Lenore made some good points. You may or may not believe in Lemuria, but I do like to think that at some point in the past, such utopian societies existed. Holding an ideal image of how we would like our world to be in our mind gives us a model to strive toward in our hectic modern life. Lenore was a peaceful person who seemed happy and when I saw her some time later, she continued to have that calm stillness that I think we would all benefit from experiencing more often in our lives.

Summing Up

I am always amazed at some of the incredible insights that come up during any session. Clients who realized their animals had come back more than once, like me, felt that they were truly blessed.

Likewise, watching a client have a revelation that they were an animal in a past life is always fascinating. Some are more surprised by their regressions than others, but regardless of how they react initially, healing is the ultimate outcome and proves that even in animal form, the soul has much to learn during each lifetime.

PART TWO

GUIDED IMAGERY JOURNEYS TO CONNECT WITH PETS AND ANIMALS

NEXT, YOU'LL HAVE SEVERAL options for connecting to your pet on a deeper level, whether you're healing from the loss of your beloved animal, or you want to better understand why you love your little fur ball so much, or you'd like to find out how you knew each other in the past. I hope you enjoy the following section.

One of the best ways to experience these exercises is to download an app on your phone or device and record them yourself, and then play them back whenever you need. Your subconscious mind loves the sound of your voice and listening to recordings can be incredibly helpful in healing and self-discovery.

For these exercises, please remember to select a quiet location, free of distractions. I recommend sitting up in a chair, but if you want to lie down, that's fine, too, so long as you don't go to sleep. With all guided journeys, there's an element of creativity involved. At times, you may be going through something and a strange thought pops into your mind. You might feel like what you're getting is silly, ridiculous even, and it couldn't possibly be real. Remember to acknowledge your feelings about that, but give yourself permission to see what the experience can reveal about your journey. It's coming up for a reason!

Part of the success of guided imagery processes involves your willingness to drop judgment and go with the flow, see what happens, and allow the deeper part of your soul to speak to you without attempting to edit yourself or pushing those insights away by dismissing them as nonsensical.

Each journey guides you into a time in your past lives, but as you noticed in the earlier sections of the book, sometimes when you go in seeking one answer, you'll find out something you didn't expect. For example, let's say you intended to discover how you and your favorite dog knew each other before, but when you take the journey, you find yourself in a completely unrelated time in your past lives. If this happens, that's fine. There's always a reason certain memories pop up. Your subconscious mind and Higher Self always present what is for your highest good at any given moment, so take it in stride, but know there's a reason for everything.

When I first became interested in hypnotherapy, I had unresolved grief to deal with, but it took quite a while to get to the root cause and solve the problem. The Higher Self keeps you safe and only reveals details when you're ready. That's why you'll notice that each journey gives answers about one situation, which is why you would benefit from recording the journeys yourself, then using them more than one time whenever you feel guided and ready to receive further information. If you don't find answers to what you're looking for the first time, don't give up. Keep going.

In my earlier book *Meet Your Karma*, I advised readers to keep a journal of experiences, and for all the reasons mentioned above, the same applies to keeping track of your pet exercises. While the idea of exploring our connections to our pets is a fun and interesting process, this can also be quite a learning experience. You never know what you might uncover that could provide a key to your soul development and personal growth. Especially when you find surprises you had no idea about, think of those insights and epiphanies as keys to unlock the wealth of information about your soul and your soul's journey. Everything is important, even seemingly inconsequential details. When you record your experiences in a journal, you can glance back later and watch the progress you've made toward self-understanding.

Regression has helped me so much through the years and I've seen these processes work wonders for others, too, so I know you have the ability to gain amazing knowledge about yourself over time and all will be for the best on your path. Above all else, enjoy the journey!

Chapter Five

_____

HEALING EXPERIENCES WITH ANIMALS

IN THIS CHAPTER YOU will explore several different ways to heal your heart when grieving the loss of a pet. Because of my own journey, I've also included a powerful exercise to help relieve fear of animals. We all know that some fear keeps us safe but if your terror has taken over your life, I hope this exercise will help you. Once that's done, you'll continue the chapter by finding new ways to work with animals and experience meeting your own Animal Spirit Guides.

Another helpful process is learning how to communicate with your pet so you know what they need, then the chapter will wrap up with a list of spiritual tools I've found helpful in working with animals. Ready? Let's get started!

Grief Recovery Journey for Loss of Your Pet

Earlier in the book during the case study about my client Misty, I mentioned the idea that we are all connected and that there's a part of you that is connected to everyone in the world. When things aren't going the way you'd like, you can do guided imagery to heal the part of you that's someone else. Normally we do this for people by visualizing them in front of us and asking for or sending forgiveness. When you do this and send healing light to another person in your imagination they actually receive the benefits, and often the difficult relationship or painful situation can be remedied in an energetic and nonverbal way.

Since our pets are not normally the source of any angst, in this book the only similar way to heal the part of us that is our pet is through the grief recovery process. Pets are part of our family; they provide us with the most authentic sense of unconditional love we will ever experience during our lifetimes. Grieving over our pets is not only natural but justified.

This next exercise will help you have a visual and kinesthetic experience of reconnecting with a lost pet on an energetic level and healing the part of you that is your lost pet, so hopefully your grief will be somewhat lessened and the pain of the loss easier to bear.

EXERCISE

Sit in a comfortable place with your feet flat on the floor and your hands in your lap. Close your eyes. Breathe in through your nose, breathing in peace and relaxation, and exhale any tension. Imagine with each breath taken that you are becoming more relaxed.

Imagine there is a beautiful light coming down from above that moves through the top of your head, into your spine, and flows through your legs and out the soles of your feet. The light carries away any tension from your day and sends it out through your feet into the earth where it can be transmuted into a healing, loving light in our earth.

Very good.

Notice that light begins to surround your body and creates a ball of bright white light that surrounds you by several feet. Floating inside this light, you feel relaxed, safe, and secure.

Imagine there is a doorway in front of you. See this door, feel it, or just know the door is there. Go ahead and open the door and step inside a beautiful room. This room may be a familiar place where you've been before, or it might be new, but either way, notice the wonderful energy you feel here.

On the other side of the room, there's another doorway there. Imagine that door is opening and that your long-lost pet walks or floats through that door. Imagine how good he or she looks, as though they are in perfect health, experiencing vitality and energy. Notice your pet is so vivid, it's as if they never, ever left you.

Go ahead and walk or float up to your pet. Talk to them and tell them how much you missed them. Imagine you can feel their fur, hear the sound they make when they're happy, and experience their unconditional love.

Now imagine picking them up or putting your arms around their neck. Allow every single cell in your body to open, expand and relax as you reconnect with your beloved pet. Starting from the tips of your toes, cells are expanding and relaxing, totally reconnecting with your pet. Very good.

Feel that light and energy moving into your feet, through your heels and ankles, up your calves, reconnecting now. Cells are relaxing and remembering a time in the past when your pet was still here and knowing your pet has now returned and all is well. All stress associated with your loss is releasing as this new energy moves into your thighs, up into your back, through your lungs, into your heart. Notice your heart expanding and relaxing, feel the amazing unconditional love of your dear pet. Feel their furry face against you, sensing the deep love and high regard your pet feels for you, knowing all is well.

Allow that feeling to continue as cells relax and expand and that light energy moves into your shoulders, arms, wrists, hands, fingers, and moves up, up, up, into your neck and shoulders and into your head. Stay there where you are, hugging your pet, relaxing in this new energy of knowing they are right here, right now. They've never left you. Notice how much better you feel knowing they're here with you again. Very good.

Take your time. Spend all the time you need reconnecting with your pet's loving energy. Know that at any time you want, you can come back into this space and meet with your dear pet once more to receive this connection and comfort.

When you're ready, imagine you can release your embrace. Notice how much lighter and brighter you feel, and how much lighter your pet looks and feels. Very good. Imagine your pet can show you, or tell you through whatever means they're able to, that you are loved. Tell your pet how much you love him or her also and imagine they get the message. Bask in this loving energy for as long as you need.

While you do, imagine that you notice a trash can near you and go ahead now and put any sadness or grief you felt before into that trash can. Fill the can up with grief, sadness, loneliness, anger, or any other emotions surrounding your pet's death that no longer serve you. Imagine this can has unlimited capacity and will carry anything you are ready to release. Very good. Do that now, releasing all the painful emotions while you fill up that can. Go ahead and continue to embrace your loving pet. Do this for as long as you need, until you feel better.

Then, when you're ready, imagine you notice there is an energetic cord of light connecting you with all the items you released into the trash can. In a moment, when I count to three, you will imagine that a big pair of golden scissors floats down and cuts that cord, releasing you forever from those emotions you're leaving behind. Ready? One, two, and three, cutting that cord. As you do, that filled trash can lifts up into the air and blasts into outer space, totally freeing and releasing you from those unwanted emotions. A gorgeous beam of light comes down through that light cord and fills your heart, your neck and shoulders, your arms, hands, fingers, legs and feet, and moves into your mind, bringing you a wonderful feeling of peace. Allow that peaceful light to move over your sweet pet, healing and continuing to restore them to optimal health and vitality.

Notice now that you have completely removed heavy emotions of grief and sadness and you've totally reconnected with your pet. Notice how good you feel and how happy the two of you are together. Very good! Now imagine your cherished friend lets you know once more how deeply you are loved and then your pet begins to walk or float back through the door from where they came, sending you an amazing feeling of love. Know that you can carry this feeling with you wherever you go.

Turn around and walk out the door where you came in and be back where you started, feeling better than you did before. In a moment when I count down from three, you will come back, feeling awake, refreshed, or better than you did before. Three, continuing to process this energy in your dreams tonight so by tomorrow morning, you will be fully integrated into your new way of being; two, noticing how much better you feel knowing your pet is in your heart always and you can easily connect to their loving energy; one, grounded, centered, and balanced; and you're back!

How did that go? I do a similar process with clients who lose a loved one and I think this works well because the most painful part of the grieving process happens when you feel the dramatic and shocking disconnect to the one you lost, so when you can reconnect with your loved one on an energetic level, or in this case with your pet, once you realize that the separation is an illusion, you start to feel better. By "illusion" I mean that our souls are infinite and death does not mean our beloved vanishes, they simply change form. This experience assists you in connecting to your beloved pet in their new form, rather than in the physical form you were used to experiencing. Remember you can close your eyes anytime and your little one is only a thought away!

Earlier in the case studies section, I had several clients go through cord cutting processes and I promised you would have a chance to do the same. In this journey, you had a chance to release emotional garbage, so to speak, that you no longer needed and then cut cords with that unwanted energy. Cord cutting is an amazing way to create healing in the body, mind, and spirit by allowing you to release anything that is no longer serving you; in this case, grief.

Grieving is a challenging process every person alive will go through in some form or another during their lives. One guided journey may or may not help you, depending on how long it's been since your loss and the depth of your sorrow.

It's hard to say when or how grief may finally feel relieved. In many cases, you simply cannot get over the loss of a loved one, but in time, by using healing processes such as the one above, you can hopefully come to a place of greater acceptance and peace about those whom you've loved and lost. I hope that's the case for you as you go through this journey, and as with all of the processes in the book, feel free to repeat the exercise so you can meet your sweet pet as many times as necessary to find the feeling of healing and relief.

Journey to Relieve Fear of Animals

Earlier I mentioned my severe dog phobia that was relieved by a helpful past life regression. Logically and obviously, some fear is built into our DNA to keep us safe and sound, but when fears become paralyzing, guided imagery can be helpful.

There's also a saying about animals that they can sense fear and will often react negatively to people they sense don't like them or who feel apprehensive toward them. For that reason, I offer this next journey to help peel back some of the outer layers of anxieties you may have about certain species. Like any process, the journey toward healing can often take a while, but my hope is that this will assist you in changing your energy just enough so that any fear currently paralyzing you or limiting your life in any way can be relieved.

EXERCISE

Find a comfortable place to sit where you won't be disturbed. With your hands resting comfortably and feet flat on the floor, close your eyes. Breathe in peace and healing and relaxation. Exhale any tension and concerns. Very good.

While you continue to breathe, imagine that with every breath you are becoming more and more relaxed. Notice a beam of pure white light is coming down from above and feel that loving light as it moves into your head, traveling down through your face and neck into your arms and hands, moving quickly down your spine. Feel the warmth of the light as it moves into your heart, calming you, relaxing and healing you as it travels into your lungs and down to the base of your spine, moving into your legs and down and out the soles of your feet.

Allow the light to heal anything that needs attention at this time and the light becomes stronger and stronger, pouring out of your head. The light forms a protective shield of light that surrounds you in all directions. Imagine you feel yourself sitting inside this light shield, feeling safer and more secure than ever before. Very good.

Go ahead and notice a doorway in front of you. Open that door and step into your beautiful room. This may be a place where you've been before, or it may be new. Either way, notice how relaxed you feel. Still surrounded by protective light, walk further into the room and imagine a beautiful angel or guide is floating down to greet you. This angel knows everything about your soul and your journey. Take a moment now and speak to the angel about any conscious fears you have of any mammals, birds, insects, or reptiles. Notice how supportive your angel is in listening to your feelings. Take your time. You may also talk about any incidents in the past that still trouble you.

When you're finished, imagine your angel tells you that they are here for you to help you heal from this situation. With that loving light surrounding you and with your angel by your side, notice another door on the other side of the room is opening and that animal or species is walking or floating through the door. This may be the same exact animal you encountered earlier, or it might be a representative of that species. Either way, know this is the Higher Self of that animal. The aspect of the animal that is all-knowing, the soul-leveled part.

If needed, imagine the animal's Higher Self wants to apologize to you for any injuries, real or imagined, that happened to you in the past. Notice they are quite sincere in this and they're saying they truly did not mean any harm. Perhaps they were also frightened and unsure of the situation. Allow the animal to explain any of this to you. Take your time. Feel free to ask any questions for clarification.

When you're done listening and talking, imagine this animal is asking you for forgiveness. Imagine that you can, with this new information, forgive the animal. Do that now. Notice there is an energetic cord between the two of you and in a moment, your angel will cut that cord. Ready? One two, three, and cut! Releasing you from the energy of the past, you and the animal are now receiving a bright healing light that washes down over the two of you, carrying away any animosity or fear you have of each other, and bringing you both into a neutral energy of mutual respect. Feel that neutrality now. Notice how good it feels to be free of these negative emotions.

To ensure you feel better, your angel is coming in now with a big trash can. Go ahead and reach inside yourself and if there's any leftover fear or negative emotions around this creature, put those feelings out now, taking them from your body and throwing them away in the trash. Take your time. Notice as you release this excess energy how much lighter and brighter you feel. Very good. Take your time. Allow your angel to assist you in any way you need. The animal is also sending you loving encouragement as you release this energy. Notice with every breath you take, you are becoming lighter and lighter, brighter and brighter. Very good.

When you're finished, notice a beam of light connecting you with this trash. On the count of three, your angel will cut this cord and free you from this unwanted energy. One, two, and three, cutting that cord and noticing it flying off into the air, into outer space where it vanishes forever, transforming into a million fragments of light that become a new loving part of the Universe. Notice how much better you feel. Good job.

If you'd like, imagine you can ask the animal now to explain to you the lessons you learned together as souls. What lesson did your former fear bring to you in your life? Notice the good things that came from this uncomfortable situation and know that now you can move forward with greater peace and neutrality toward this animal.

Take your time, discuss anything else you need to with your angel or the animal and when you're ready, imagine the animal walks, floats, or flies back through that door. Thank your angel for helping you today, then watch them float away.

Turn and walk out the door where you came in and be there now, back where you started. When I count down from three, you will be back in the room, fully awake, feeling better than before. Three, finding peace toward the former fear of the animal you just met; two, finding that peace expanding in your life and noticing how your entire life improves as a result of this new understanding; one, feeling stronger and more self-assured than ever before, grounded, centered and balanced; and you're back!

Now that you know where your fear comes from regarding a certain kind of animal or species, you can use this information in another exercise in the next chapter to go deeper into your exploration and clearing of the issue.

Journey to Discover Animal Totems and Animal Spirit Guides

Early in my spiritual journey, I was introduced to one of my favorite books of all time, Llewellyn's *Animal Speak* by the late, great Ted Andrews. Through that writing, I learned about the power of totem animals. The book opened my mind to the idea that my dog attack mentioned earlier might mean that rather than being my enemy, the dog actually might be one of my guides and teachers. Once I used that knowledge to do some journey work, I began having dreams about a gorgeous grey wolf. My fear of dogs lessened over time, and I began viewing dogs as spiritual medicine, and that shift in thinking created a vast difference in my attitude.

During my healing past life regression where I identified my past life connection with dogs, I had another insight about the wolf I'd been seeing in my meditations. I always believed it was some kind of Native American totem, but now I knew this was one of the huskies from those very early times. The wolf did not look exactly like a typical prairie wolf, nor did it appear to be exactly like the huskies we see today. It was something different. Breeding makes subtle changes over time and after some research, I found a photo of an animal that looks quite similar to the one in my vision called a Norwegian elkhound, which is stockier than the typical husky and in some regards looks a little like the German shepherd that bit me when I was a child. Coincidence? I think not!

Part of any past life regression involves introducing clients to a helpful guide or an angel who can accompany them on their journey. Having someone go with you while you discover new things about yourself can be a real comfort. Typically, people identify these helpers as angels. At other times, clients say the assistant is a guide, and on less-common occasions, clients journeyed into spaces where they met animals who assisted them on the path of healing. The following case histories are some of my favorite examples.

I'm convinced that we all have Animal Spirit Guides who are somehow cosmically assigned to work with us. We may acknowledge those helpers when we see them out in nature, as the *Animal Speak* book suggests, or we may seek them out in meditation. Either way, animals provide incredible wisdom if we will only open our minds to the possibilities.

Have you wondered what animals are guiding you in your current life? Now you'll have a chance to find out. In this journey you will travel to a space where you will have a visionary encounter with the primary creatures assisting you from the spirit world. We all have guides, yet typically we perceive them as angels or ascended masters. Some of our most powerful helpers are the energies of the natural world.

EXERCISE

Find a comfortable place to sit where you won't be disturbed. Perhaps you have a special place you go. I recommend using the same place each time to cue your subconscious mind to prepare for your journey. Breathe in and out through your nose. Imagine with every breath you feel more and more relaxed. Allow a bright healing light to move from the top of your head, through your scalp, face, neck, arms, and hands, moving down your spine, through your heart and lungs to your lower back as it continues into your legs and feet. Allow this light to relax you and notice now that it expands to form a ball of protective light around your body. Very nice.

Imagine a door in front of you. Open that door and find yourself stepping out into a beautiful place in nature. A place that you love and feel comfortable and safe. Notice if this is a sunny or a cloudy day. Are you in the mountains? At the beach? Allow whatever happens to happen and know all is well. Walk or float through this gorgeous setting and as you do, you notice a tree up ahead. Notice what kind of tree it is and go ahead now and either lean against it or sit under it. Feel the loving energies of the tree and the safety and security your tree provides.

Off in the distance you notice something moving toward you. It gets closer and you soon see your Spirit Animal walking, flying, or floating over to you. Allow your Spirit Animal to come up to you and say hello. Go ahead now and ask questions.

How long has this guide been with you? What lessons are you here to learn from your special Spirit Animal? How does your Spirit Animal assist you in daily life? Are there new ways your animal would like to communicate with you? If so, what are those? Take your time and allow your animal to tell you all you need to know at this time. Very good.

When you're ready, imagine your Spirit Animal walks or floats away. Know that if you need additional guidance you can return to this place and your Spirit Animal will be more than happy to assist. Feel the unconditional love and high regard your animal has for you and thank him or her for being with you today. Once they disappear, move away from your tree and walk or float back to the door where you entered. With every step you take, you feel more relaxed than you did before you arrived. Go ahead now and open the door, stepping back out to where you started.

In a moment, when I count down from three, you will arrive back in the room, feeling awake, refreshed, and better than you did before. Ready? Three, processing the details from your visit with your Spirit Animal in your dreams tonight so by tomorrow morning, you are fully integrated into this new energy; two, driving safe and being safe in all activities; one, grounded, centered, and balanced; and you're back!

How did that go? Feel free to write about your Animal Spirit Guides in a journal and know you can contact them throughout your life to provide healing and guidance on all of life's challenges.

Pet Communication Experience

Now that you've had a chance to tap into your Animal Spirit Guides, this next exercise will help you communicate better with the real-life animals that surround you on a daily basis. I've had the privilege to be called in as a pet communicator in the past to do healings on all kinds of pets, from dogs and cats to horses and birds. What I've found is that the majority of time owners need help is when they are overly concerned to the point where they can no longer hear their own inner guidance. You know your pet better than anyone, and yet just like any relationship, sometimes when we're in the middle of it, we can't see the solutions that are right in front of us.

The best example I have is when I was called out to a vet's office to visit a schnauzer who stopped eating when his owners went on vacation. The moment I arrived, I connected with his Higher Self because yes, dogs, cats, and other animals also have a Higher Self, as you experienced earlier in the Animal Spirit exercise. I asked the dog what I could do to help him feel happier, then I waited for the answer. It was fairly simple: He told me in my mind that he wanted to go stay with the neighbors and didn't like being in a cage. I called the owner and she made arrangements for him to be picked up. Sure enough, he was eating and drinking again in no time.

I was credited with providing some kind of miraculous healing, which I do not believe was warranted. We can all tune in to our furry friends and know what's best if we only calm ourselves enough to receive the answers. When you're worried and upset about your fur baby, it can become quite a disruption to your routine. If BisKit needs something and I can't figure out how to help him, I drop everything until I find answers. We all need help once in a while. What I hope is that this next exercise will help you find answers within your Higher Self. I'll show you how easy it is to connect to your animals and become the dog, cat, or horse whisperer you've always wanted to be.

EXERCISE

Sit comfortably and close your eyes. Breathe in peace and relaxation, exhale tension and concern. Imagine as you breathe, your pet can float up in front of you. Know that this is your pet's Higher Self, their soul, and not who they are physically. Greet your pet, allow your pet to send you love. Go ahead and receive that, sending them love back. Very good.

If there's a challenge with your pet, ask the Higher Self how you can best help them at this time. Be still and quiet and wait for the answer. You may hear the answer in your mind, you may see a visual picture, or you may have an inner knowing. Allow those thoughts and feelings to emerge from something beyond yourself. It may even feel like you're making this up, but that's good. Simply allow.

Take your time and once you're done, ask your pet's Higher Self if there's anything else they'd like to tell you at this time. They might want to talk about their food, bedding, other animals or people, or they may want to simply love you. Whatever it is, be open to receiving whatever comes through at this time.

Allow your pet to express themselves until they have discussed everything they wanted to share. Thank your pet for speaking with you today. When you're ready, open your eyes and come back.

Now that you've done this process, the true test is to go into the outer world and take actions in accordance to whatever thoughts, images, or feelings you received. Did your pet complain about their food? Did they request something new? If so, give them what they asked for and see how things change and, hopefully, improve.

Part of success in any form of intuitive guidance is to treat the information not as some figment of your abundant imagination, but as a true statement of fact. Act on what you receive as though you came to this information from your regular senses and then wait a period of time to see what changes occur. Hopefully things improve in a way that is quick and noticeable.

Since I'm a cat owner, I use the food as an example. Dogs are wonderfully open to anything they get to eat, but cats, as I'm sure you know, are picky and particular. Food is a simple way to test your connection to your pet because it's easy to fix. If your pet wanted tuna instead of chicken for example, then go for it! The change won't cost much, so do as you're guided and see how things shift. Your dog may want to ride in the car or have more table scraps. Whatever you came up with is awesome! Just be sure and take your own advice and you'll find that next time there's a crisis, you can tune in yourself and won't have to call in a pet detective to get to the bottom of what's going on with your baby. Try this! It works!

Spiritual Tools for Working with Your Pet

My work combines energy healing with the past life regression process because thoughts are things and they occupy physical space in our energetic fields. I am particularly well versed in the use of gems and stones to shift energy and I've found that pets respond well to stones when they're placed in and around their bedding area. Sometimes the stones can be quite helpful additions to speaking to your pet because stones shift energy and can assist your pet in making needed changes and do so in a very gentle way. Here are a few of the best stones you can use with your pets:

Amethyst

Amethyst is a gorgeous purple stone that resonates to the frequency of the violet ray, and as such, has a very high frequency. The stone is gentle yet subtly lifts lower vibrations up and away from your animal simply by placing a piece in the room (or, in the case of a horse, the stall) of your pet. You can also give your pet an energetic bath by waving your stone about an inch over their physical body to help shift energy.

Some animals are super sensitive to this, though, so use your intuition and you may find that simply placing the stone in the area where you pet sits or sleeps is enough to set the intentions for feeling better and making positive change.

Rose Quartz

Rose quartz is a gentle pink stone that opens the heart and reflects loving kindness, sending out a warm energy to your pet. I recommend placing the stone near the bed for best results.

Crystal

Clear quartz crystal is a transmitter of energy and can get stagnant vibrations when moving into higher realms. If you have smaller crystals, you can create a grid by encircling your pet's bed with the crystals so an energetic ball of light is created that will help tremendously.

Dogs react better than cats to the grid, though. Cats are so picky they may reject a bed that's been shifted in this way. They do feel the energy! Your dog, on the other hand, is often more open to your suggestion.

For horses, place the crystals in the four corners of the stall and imagine a ball of light surrounding them, healing and calming them. Any of these listed stones in a stall can assist, but if your horse is lethargic, the clear crystal is best.

Selenite

When BisKit came home from the animal shelter after I first adopted him, he became ill, so I used several different stones to help him. The ones he resonated best with were my selenite wands, which are long shards I placed around his bed in a square formation. I have photos of my little darling resting his head and stretching out on the selenite, and sure enough, he made a speedy recovery. Selenite is a great stone for cleansing all the energy fields of the body, for people and pets too!

Sage & Salt

The other thing to keep in mind is that your pet is an extension of you. Are you stressed beyond belief? Are you stuffing down your feelings and emotions, then wondering why your baby isn't well? At times, you should attempt to stop the madness of the outer world, close your eyes, and do some deep healing and calming breathing. Once you feel more relaxed yourself, you may notice your pet also calms down. Of course, that may be easier said than done. If that's the case, a couple of my other favorite tools are sage and salt.

Sage

Sage is an herb bundled up with string that you can light and use to clear a room. If your space is feeling constrictive or you're super stressed out, you can smudge your area with a sage wand, walking room to room as you think peaceful thoughts. While doing so, please remember to smudge your pet's bedding and areas where your dear animals like to stay. Afterward, you may also open all the windows, allowing fresh air to permeate your space as the winds of change blow in a new refreshing energy. Your pets will feel the new energy and the intentions you're putting out to make your environment more peaceful; they will also calm down.

Salt

I love to work with different kinds of salt as a protective tool. Common table salt can be great for encircling a perimeter around your home to cast a protective glow around your property. Likewise, you can walk room to room inside the house and put a dash of salt in each corner of a room to protect the energy and remove unwanted influences.

Epsom salts are comprised of magnesium sulfide and are also helpful for removing lower-frequency vibrations. I love bathing in Epsom salts because they clear your energetic field. I don't recommend bathing pets in them, but if you cleanse yourself, your pet will receive the benefits.

Salts are magical and can be quite beneficial for setting a calm and sacred space you and your pet can enjoy. I'm reminded of my recent trip to a meditation center. We were in deep trance for ten days and mentally I was incredibly far away from my normal focus in the outer world. When I returned home, poor little BisKit had caught a cold and he had apparently felt miserable the whole time I was gone. I think this is because your animal is psychically connected to you all the time, but when you're not on the planet, which I was not, you disconnect and that is upsetting. After a few days of snuggling and tuning back in to BisKit, he fortunately got better.

What was weird is that I've been gone for months at a time, yet this shorter trip seemed to affect him more profoundly than the longer ones because I was mentally further away. I've actually been overseas at times when his furry little face pops into my mind's eye, and that's how I connect with him when I'm gone—through the dream state. This is easy to do with a cat since they sleep twenty-plus hours a day. During my recent meditation course, I did not connect with BisKit at all, hence his physical distress.

Keep this in mind with your pets, and I know you'll see positive results. We are connected to everyone, yet we have a super special connection with our furry kids.

Summing Up

Journal about the experiences and see where they take you as part of the puzzle pieces of the soul. We spend a lifetime attempting to figure out why we're here and what our bigger purpose is for being. These journeys will hopefully provide helpful clues along the path.

Chapter Six

PAST LIFE CLEARINGS

NEXT UP, WE WILL do the exercises you've been waiting for and uncover the past life connections you share with your pets using a variety of different strategies. The first journey will help you identify whether or not any of your pets from your current life have come back to you more than once, then you'll have a chance to explore connections to your favorite animals from lives you lived long ago. You'll also explore whether or not you've ever had a past life in animal form and have a chance to see yourself in a mirror. The results may surprise you.

We will end the guided journeys by taking you into a space where you can tap into deep feelings of love for your pet and transfer that loving vibration out to the world around you. Ready?

Coming Back—Discovering Pets Who Returned in Your Current Lifetime

The love affair you have with a pet can go beyond most relationships you have in your life. There's a connection there, a deep understanding and a feeling of unconditional love pets give that is unlike any other relationship.

Unlike people, our pets are here for such a short period of time, could it be possible you've crossed paths with your pet in an earlier time in your current life? And if so, what lessons are your souls learning together? That's what you're about to find out in this next exercise.

EXERCISE

Sit in a comfortable space where you'll have time to relax and close your eyes. Begin to breathe in through your nose, imagining your breath is sending you into a state of deep rest. Notice as before that you can feel a beautiful light that moves through your head, neck, and shoulders and travels down through your arms, spine, and legs and into your feet. Imagine the light is washing away any stress, making you feel relaxed and peaceful. Very good. Allow the light to move through you and surround you, shielding you from the outer world. Know that you are floating now, inside a healing ball of light and that within the light, all is well. You are safe, secure, and peaceful. Very nice.

Go ahead and notice a doorway in front of you and walk or float through that doorway now. Find yourself inside a familiar space in your home that feels safe and comfortable. This may be an indoor space or it may be outside. Pay attention to what you notice and know all is well.

Take a look around and see one of your animals walking up to you. Say hello, pet your animal, and relate to them as you normally would. Imagine this animal has a reason to come here today in order to answer an important question for you: Have you been together before in this current lifetime? Yes or no? Imagine your beloved animal can answer by giving you an inner feeling of that answer.

If it's a yes, notice the prior animal can walk or float over to you now. Take a look, listen to how they both sound, or have an inner sense of the familiarity between these two pets. How are they similar? How are they different? What lessons are the two of you learning together in these two embodiments? What lessons are you learning through these varied experiences and why have your souls chosen to be together? Imagine it is easy for you to understand all the reasons.

Take your time to feel the energy of your pet, particularly any who have crossed over to the other side. Feel the love they still have for you and know that the connection and that love never disappears. What benefits have you realized from receiving and giving this unconditional love?

Notice in this safe space that there's a computer screen there. Ask your beloved pet if your souls have been together in past lifetimes too. Yes or no? If yes, imagine that the screen begins to broadcast a video showing you the lifetime where you knew each other before. Watch this video and know all there is to know about that very early time. What year in the past did you know your pet? How has your relationship evolved through the years? What lessons did you learn together in that past life and why was it important to revisit you in your current lifetime? Take your time and pay attention to what you notice. Allow the video to play as long as needed to show you, tell you, or give you an inner feeling of all you learned through this loving relationship.

When you're ready, notice that video turns off and you can easily bring your attention back into the room with your beloved pet or pets. Ask if there's anything else they want you to know at this time. Tell them anything you want to say. When you're finished, imagine they walk or float away saying, "I love you," as they leave. Continue basking in their love and carry those wonderful feelings with you as you turn and walk out the door.

Find yourself back where we started, still surrounded by protective light, knowing you are safe and secure, and that all is well. In a moment, when I count down from three, you will come back into the room, feeling awake, refreshed, and better than you did before. Three, processing this information in your dreams so by tomorrow morning you are fully aware of this new information; two, driving safe, being safe in all activities; one, continuing to feel the effects of this profound, unconditional love and carrying that with you during the coming days, weeks, and months; and you're back!

How did that go? Were you able to uncover the connection to pets you've had during different times in your life? Was it something you'd considered before, or did you receive new information? This journey is definitely worth writing about, so if anything particularly meaningful happened, take notes. Remember that more might float in later, when you least expect it, or you may have a dream about your pets that gives you even more information. Above all, I hope you felt the love of your pet and can tap into that feeling whenever you need encouragement.

Discovering Past Lives with Your Pets

Since you may have had several pets during your lifetime, feel free to use this same process as much as you would like. The difference will be in the intention you set when you begin. For example, I could imagine the cat I have right now, then close my eyes and go through the process, or I could begin by thinking about and concentrating on the pet I had when I was a child.

Even when you set an intention, be prepared for surprises. At times, you'll never know what might come up when you go through the process, and that's part of the fun. Your soul is a vast wellspring of energy and information, so do your best to be open-minded. On the other hand, you may not want to set any intention at all, and that's fine too.

You may be like me and you've had so many pets through the years, you can simply ask your Higher Self to provide the information most needed at this moment and know all is well. Ready?

EXERCISE

Sit in a comfortable place where you won't be disturbed and close your eyes. Breathe in peace, and healing, and relaxation; exhale tension and concern. Know as you continue breathing that with every single breath you take, you are becoming more and more relaxed. Very good.

Notice a beam of pure white light coming down through the top of your head. Feel that light moving into your head, flowing down into your neck and shoulders; it continues moving down your spine, into your arms, hands, and fingers, and down into your legs and feet. Allow the light to become so strong, it begins to pour out of your heart, creating a beautiful green ball of light that surrounds you by a foot in all directions. Feel yourself floating in this green healing light, knowing that within the light, only that which is of your highest good can come through.

Notice there is a doorway in front of you. When I count to three, you will open the door. Ready? One, two, and three: open the door. Step outside into a beautiful place in nature. Notice how relaxed you feel as you look around. Notice the sky, notice if there are any trees, or animals; allow yourself to feel completely relaxed in the warm embrace of this natural space. Very good.

Imagine as you take in the natural beauty, a beloved pet or animal you've known in your current life will either walk or float up to you or they may float down from above. Whichever way they arrive, allow it to happen so by the time I count to three that animal will be with you. One, two, three, they're with you now. Very good. Notice which animal showed up and thank them for being here today.

Your beloved animal is here with you today to help you uncover the deeper connection the two of you share. Imagine this is your animal friend's soul or Higher Self and this animal knows everything there is to know about the two of you and the past you've shared. They can easily speak to you telepathically through their thoughts and show you important lessons about the connection you share.

Imagine you can take your animal in your arms or wrap your arms around their neck and the two of you will begin now to float. Lifting up, up, up, higher and higher into the clouds, floating out of the beautiful place in nature, you find yourself now floating in the sky, in light, fluffy clouds. Totally relaxed and carefree, knowing that the higher up you float, the more relaxed you feel.

Imagine you and your pet have floated so high in the sky that as you look down you notice a gentle stream of water below you. Imagine you are floating over today and you can turn and look back toward your past. Very nice.

In a moment when I count to three, you and your animal are going to float into the past to the source event, to the very first time you met or to the most important event in the past where you've known each other before. Ready? One two, three… floating back, back, back, go way, way back, into the past. When I count to three you will arrive at this very early time. One, floating back; two, further and further; and three. You're there. Be there now and notice what's happening. What year is this; the first thing that comes to your mind? Where are you? Are you alone or with other people? Imagine you can forward to an event where you and your animal were together. Be there now. What's happening?

Continue to experience these events for as long as you need. When you're ready, imagine you can fast-forward to the very last day of that lifetime and be there now. Notice how you pass into spirit. Still surrounded by the green healing light, lift yourself up, out of that body, and go into the peaceful space between lives. Be there now. So, what lessons did you learn in that lifetime? How did you grow as a result of the relationship you had with your animal? What lessons did the two of you come to learn together as souls and how does that relate to your current lifetime?

Take your time to receive this information. When you're ready, imagine you can lift higher, up, up, up, and find yourself back, over the line of light, over that very early time.

In a moment when I count to three, you will begin floating back, allowing all events between that very early time and now to receive new healing and light because of this information. Ready? One, floating back toward today; two, moving quickly toward the current day; and three, be there now. Very good.

Imagine you can ask your beloved animal if there are any other messages they have for you about your journey together as souls. Take your time. When you're ready, take your animal in your arms, or hold them tight as the two of you float down, down, down, back through the clouds, until you land, back in that beautiful place in nature where you began.

Thank your dear animal friend for assisting you in this way. Know you can return here anytime for healing and further insights. Allow your animal to say goodbye for now and watch as they walk or float away. Feel the unconditional love and high regard they have for you. Very nice. Now turn and walk back through the doorway where we began. You find yourself back in the place where you started, still surrounded by the green healing light, knowing that within this protective healing light, only that which is of your highest good can come through.

In a moment, when I count down from three, you will return feeling awake, refreshed, and better than you did before. Ready? Three, processing this information in your dreams tonight so by tomorrow morning you are in full alignment with this new energy and information; two, driving safe and being safe in all activities; one, grounded centered, and balanced; and you're back!

How did that go? Were you surprised by what you discovered? You may want to make some notes in your journal and notice if you have any dreams or insights in the coming days and weeks.

Past Lives with Other Animals Journey

Throughout human history, animals played an important role. No doubt you've had past lives where animals proved a significant part of your journey, and in this next process, you'll have a chance to discover which animals were with you and why.

EXERCISE

Take a seat or lay down in a comfortable place where you can relax. Close your eyes. Take a deep breath in through your nose, breathing in peace, healing, and relaxation, and exhaling tension. Very good. Notice that familiar beam of healing light is moving through the top of your head, moving into your neck and shoulders, moving down through your arms and hands, into your heart, traveling down your spine into your legs and feet. Feel the light rushing through you allowing you to feel relaxed. Soon that light begins to surround you, so you find yourself now floating in a ball of pure white light. Know that within the light you will receive truth and healing and know that all is well.

Notice a doorway in front of you, open that door and step into a peaceful space. This might be a place you've been to before, or it could be new. Know that you are safe and secure here and allow yourself to relax even more. As you do, a beautiful angel or Spirit Guide floats down to join you. Know that this guide has come to assist you today in accessing details for your soul development. Go with your guide now and float into the air, through the ceiling of this space, float into the clouds, moving higher and higher, up, up, up, moving away from daily concerns to access the realm of the spirit. You are floating so high now, you realize you're above a line of light that represents your soul journey. You're floating over today. In a moment, your guide will accompany you back into your past to a very early time when animals played an important role in your life lessons. Ready? Float back now, moving quickly into the past to a time before your current life. In a moment, when I count to three, you will arrive. One, floating back; two, further and further; and three, you're there. Be there now; float down into that very early time and notice what's happening.

What year is this? Where are you? Are you a man or woman? What's happening? Experience several events and watch while the scene unfolds. What animals are there? Why are they important? Imagine it's easy to know and notice. Very nice.

Go ahead now and fast-forward to the very last day of your life. Be there now and pass into spirit, knowing you are still surrounded by a healing light. Move up, up, up, out of that body, into the peaceful space between lives. What lessons did you learn in the life you just visited? How did animals shape your journey? What lessons did they give you that are still important to you in your current life? Take a moment and receive any insights. Allow your guide or the animals themselves to talk to you and show you any important things you need to know at this time.

When you're ready, go ahead and float up higher, into the clouds, thanking all who assisted you in this lifetime and find yourself floating above this early time. Move toward the present day, taking all the learning you received. Find yourself now floating over today. Allow yourself to go with your guide as the two of you float down through the clouds again, coming back to earth, moving through the ceiling of the room where we started. Thank the guide for helping you today and say goodbye. Know that you can come and seek guidance in the future if needed. Watch your guide float away and then turn around to go through the door where you entered. Nice job.

Surrounded by the healing light, in a moment when I count down from three you will return, feeling awake, refreshed, and better than before. Three, recalling the healing received from the animals and feeling gratitude for the lessons; two, processing this information in your dreams so that you are integrated into the new energy by tomorrow morning; one, finding renewed appreciation for animals after this journey; and you're back!

How did that journey turn out? Which animals did you see? How did they impact your experience and soul lessons? Nice job!

Experiencing Your Past Lives in Animal Form

Earlier we heard from people who believe they lived past lives as animals, and when you think about it, that's not too hard to believe. As we discussed in part one, many religions acknowledge the idea that animals have souls and that the soul evolves into various forms during the many lives we live. In this next journey, you will have a chance to go back in time to lives where you existed in animal form. There's a chance, of course, that you'll take this journey and find out you never did have a past life as an animal, and that's fine. The journey will still give you some kind of past life experience, whether or not you pull up an animal lifetime. The soul is so vast, you always receive the information you most need at any given time. Ready?

EXERCISE

With a calm and quiet mind, take a seat in a comfortable space and close your eyes. Feel a peaceful healing light move through the top of your head and travel down into your eyes, nose, jaw, continuing down through your neck and shoulders, into your arms, elbows, wrists, hands, and fingers. Imagine the light moving through your spine into your legs and feet. Allow the light to wash away any tensions and notice that with each breath you take, you feel more and more relaxed. That loving light surrounds you now in a golden glow. Know that within this golden light you are safe and only that which is of your highest good can come through.

Imagine a doorway in front of you. This might be the same door you've walked through before, or it could be new. Open the door now and step inside a beautiful room. Feel the pleasant vibrations in this place as you start to look around. Notice now a loving angel or guide is floating down from above. Feel the unconditional love your guide has for you and imagine now that the two of you can begin to float. Floating up through the ceiling of this room, find yourselves out in the clouds, floating away and noticing that the higher up you float, the more relaxed you feel. Very good.

You and your guide are floating over today. Below you, you'll notice a white beam of light that represents time. Your guide knows all there is to know about you, so ask him or her a question—have I existed in animal form? Yes or no? Allow your mind to notice the first answer you receive. As that answer pops into your mind, find yourself floating back over that beam of light into the direction of your past. In a moment when I count to three you will arrive at this moment when you were in animal form, or if you've never been in animal form before, you will arrive at a space when animals played an important role in your soul journey. Ready? One, floating back; two, very quickly, further and further back in time; and three, you're there. Be there now and imagine you and your guide can float down through those clouds and be in this early time.

Where are you? What year is this? What kind of animal are you? Be there now, fully engaged in your life and imagine your mind can quickly recall all the details of this important time. Fast-forward quickly through your time in animal form and arrive to the very last day of that life. Still surrounded by a loving, protective light, notice how you pass into spirit and do that now. Lift up, up, up, out of that body, into the peaceful space between lives. What lessons did you learn in your life as this animal? How are those lessons playing out in your current incarnation? Why did your soul choose to become an animal? Or if you never did take animal form, why didn't you? Allow your guide to help answer these questions and know that the answers are easy to receive. Very nice.

When you're ready, go with your guide as the two of you float back down through the clouds, coming back into the beautiful room where you started. Thank your guide for joining you today and know if you need further clarification, your guide can meet you here to discuss this further.

While your guide floats away, turn and go back through the door where you entered. In a moment, when I count down from three, you'll be back, feeling refreshed and better than ever. Three, continuing to process this new information in your dreams tonight so by tomorrow morning you will be fully integrated into this energy; two, driving safely, being safe always; one, grounded, centered, and balanced; and you're back!

How did you do? Were you surprised by what you found? Did you receive relevant connections into how your life in animal form is helping with your soul growth? The soul is so vast, each time you do a journey, more is revealed. All in divine time as the information is meant for you to receive. That's why life is so interesting. Your soul is an unfolding adventure with new insights and gifts that show up along the way at the right time and place. Journaling about your experiences can be quite helpful.

Past Lives Mirror Experience

As discussed in the case history section of the book, another helpful way to experience yourself in animal form is to glance at yourself in a mirror. People sometimes have a hard time describing themselves or their past lives when they take on the animal form. This is because of a limited vocabulary and the completely different context they find themselves in as an animal rather than being human. This next exercise will help you create a more vivid image of yourself to help you uncover the meaning behind any lifetimes you've had in animal form. Ready?

EXERCISE

Sit in your comfortable spot and close your eyes. Breathe in through your nose, out through your nose, and with every breath, you find yourself becoming more and more relaxed. Allow a loving beam of pure white light to come down through the top of your head, moving into your neck, shoulders, arms, wrists, and fingertips, and continue down your spine, into your legs and feet. Allow that light to pour out of your heart, surrounding you in a bright ball of protective light. Know that within the light you are safe and secure and only that which is of your highest good can come through.

Notice a door in front of you. This may be the same door you've seen before, or it might be new. Open the door and step inside a beautiful room. Notice how relaxed and at ease you feel here. Safe and secure. As you start to look around an angel or guide floats down to meet you. This angel knows everything there is to know about you and your soul and your soul's journey. Imagine the angel is going to help you today to see who you've been before.

Imagine you and your angel can walk or float over to a wall on the other side of this room and there, you'll find a mirror. Ask your angel an important question, "Have I ever been an animal? Yes or no?"

Listen to your angel answer your question. Notice the first answer that pops into your mind. If the answer is yes, go ahead now and look into the mirror and see yourself as you've been in the past.

What animal are you? How do you feel?

Notice this mirror has a doorknob on it and turn that doorknob and step out into that lifetime when you were in animal form. Where are you? What year is this? Notice the first thing that comes into your mind.

Fast-forward through major events in your life until you arrive at the very last day of that life. Surrounded still by that lovely white healing light, notice how it is you pass away. Do that now. Go into the space between lives. What lessons did you learn in animal form? How is that life affecting your current reality? What can you learn from the experience that will make your current life better? Notice all these things, then float down, through the clouds and move back through the door where you came into this experience.

Find yourself back in the beautiful room and thank your guide or angel for assisting you today. Say goodbye as they float away. Bring all this information with you as you turn and go back through the door you came from and find yourself where you started.

In a moment, when I count down from three, you will come back feeling awake, refreshed, and better than you did before. Three, grounded centered and balanced; two, processing this in your dreams tonight so you will be fully integrated into this new energy by morning; and one, coming back!

How did you do with the mirror journey? Did you find this easier to access the animal form than the more traditional past life regression process? At times, the mirror is necessary. Even in traditional regression, the mirror can be an amazing and often startling tool to see yourself in the exact form you had in the past.

Pet Love

I hope you've had some meaningful encounters with your cherished pets during the previous guided imagery experiences. This final exercise will bring the purpose of your journeys to the forefront as you go deep within to tap into profound feelings of love, peace, and joy that come from loving an animal.

There's a saying that we need to be the change we want to see in our world. I believe that's true. One way to bring more love into your life and your world is by creating that feeling first within yourself.

We discussed early in the book that we tend to love our animals more than people at times because they offer us unconditional understanding and support. To bring profound feelings of love into our hearts so we can benefit from those feelings in other areas of life, it makes sense then to tap into the love of our pets. In this next process, you will create feelings of acceptance, love, and peace toward all sentient beings by first tapping into the love you have for your pet. To do this, you can think of one of the pets you encountered from previous journeys that you knew in past lives, or you can think of any animal you love deeply. Regardless, it should be an amazing experience. Ready?

EXERCISE

Sit in your comfortable chair and gently close your eyes. Begin breathing in peace, healing, relaxation, and joy; and exhale any tensions and concerns. Continue breathing in through your nose to the count of four—one, two, three, four. Exhaling one, two, three, and four. Very good. Keep allowing yourself to fill with peace and tranquility and exhale anything that is no longer serving you. Know that throughout this journey, every time you inhale, you will absorb love, and any time you exhale, you release stress.

Imagine there's a doorway in front of you. This may be a door you've seen before or not. Go ahead now and open that door and step inside your beautiful, safe space. Feel the amazing vibrations of your special spot as you look around. A door on the other side of the room is opening now and here comes your most cherished pet. Allow them to walk, float, or fly through the door and come to greet you now. If they've passed into spirit, notice how they look young, energized, and happy to see you.

Greet your special companion with a pat on the head, and say whatever you need to tell them now. As you do, you may wish to hug your pet. Do that now. Feel your arms wrapping around them as if they're right here, right now. Good job. Allow that feeling to sink into every single cell of your being starting with the tips of your toes. Allow your cells to expand and invite your special pet into your energy, sensing an expanded feeling of love and happiness in your body as that sensation moves up your legs, into your back and your stomach, breathing in that love through your lungs as the feeling moves up into your heart, your neck and shoulders, your arms and hands, and into your head and mind.

Bring your attention into your heart as you hold your pet and feel the love they have for you. Allow your heart energy to expand and grow. A warm sensation fills your heart and you begin to feel immense gratitude for the love you and your pet share. There's nobody in the world you love more and who loves you back. How does this feel to know you're loved so much? How do you feel opening yourself to this expanded feeling of love for others?

Now allow your mind to open up to others who may want to come through the door—family, friends, coworkers. Notice who shows up for you. See now that they, too, love you just as much as your pet. Perhaps you didn't notice that before, but allow these friends to express their gratitude for you and the role you've played in their lives. Go ahead now and tell them what they mean to you, take your time and then when you're finished, let them step aside and be there with your pet.

Your heart is opening and expanding, relaxing to the loving vibrations of knowing that you are loved and that you love others. Now imagine the door opens to your neighborhood, your city and state, your country. Feel yourself extending love to all beings in those areas. Notice how wonderful you feel as you love all life and allow life to love you back.

Imagine you are now lifting up off the ground and you're floating above this room where you started, lifting above your pet and all those who have gathered with you, you see yourself floating over your town, your city, your state, and country until you find yourself in outer space, gazing down at Mother Earth. Send love to the planet and imagine Mother Earth loves you back. See our planet as a living being and send light and gratitude.

Continue expanding yourself until you can imagine that Mother Earth fits in the palm of your hand. Hold her gently, care for her and for all the animals, people, and living beings that occupy our home. Send love and imagine you can feel love coming back to you through your hand, and that love moves up your arm into your heart. Your heart has never felt fuller and you see yourself living in harmony with all people and all beings.

Take your time, and when you're ready, begin to float back through space over the planet, over the country, your state and city, and find yourself back inside the room where we started. Imagine that all the family, friends, and neighbors who joined you today are waving goodbye, thanking you for taking the time to send them love, healing, and well wishes, and notice that they once again want to express their love for you. You matter to them! They need you and you need them and together, you can create the life you want to experience. Allow them to walk through the door where they came in originally. Notice they may be saying things like, "Thank you," or "I love you." Tell them anything you'd like to say as they go back to where they came from, feeling better than before.

Once they're all gone, the only one who remains is your special pet or pets. Go ahead and give your pet a hug again, sending them love and receiving the most profound feeling of love you've ever felt. Allow every cell in your being to really tune in to what it feels like to be so loved and needed. Gaze into your pet's eyes and you can see the love they have for you. Beginning this time with the top of your head, feel that love move into your mind, into your eyes, nose, mouth, and jaw. Allow your jaw, neck, and shoulders to relax as you bring those loving feelings into your arms—your elbows, wrists, hands, and fingertips. Pet your little animal or creature and send them love through your fingers. Very good.

Keep on allowing that loving feeling your pet is sending you to travel from your shoulders, down your neck and spine, moving one vertebrae at a time as the love moves into your heart, your stomach, and down into your lungs. Breathe in love, exhale love. Notice how much more love you have within you now than when we started so that when you breathe out, you can send love out to your pet and all other beings on our planet.

Allow this light and love to move into your legs once more, into your thighs, knees, calves, ankles, heels, and toes, and move out the soles of your feet. Send this newly increased love down, down, down, through the soles of your feet and allow it to travel deep into the core of the earth as if you're sending love directly into our planet.

While you do that, imagine roots emerge from the soles of your feet and those roots travel down, down, down into the core of our earth connecting you to our planet.

Notice how much lighter and brighter you feel as a result of giving and receiving this love. Good job! Now turn your complete focus to your lovely pet, thanking him or her for being in your life. Notice your pet is thanking you, also; not in words but in expression. Carry that feeling with you now as your pet walks back through the door where they entered. You say bye for now, knowing you can and will see your pet again, and you can easily create these loving feelings from now on, any time you think of this particular pet. If you need to in the future, you can close your eyes for a moment and find yourself in the presence of this pet, and that will instantly bring you into a feeling of peace unlike anything you've felt before. You can always carry this peace with you, throughout your day, into daily life to make your entire world feel peaceful and relaxing.

Once your pet goes through the door, turn around and find the door you originally came in. Open that door and step out into the place where you started. You feel grounded, centered, and balanced, and in a moment, when I count down from three, you will come back, feeling awake, refreshed and loved, and better than before.

Three, processing this new loving energy in your dreams so by tomorrow you will be fully integrated into this expanded, loving space; two, driving safe, being safe in all activities; one, and you're back!

How did that go? Did you find it easier to develop deep feelings of love for everyone when you thought of your pet first? Seems silly, but I've found this works because our pets are so good at loving us, we can love them back, then transfer that energy on to the world around us.

You can also do different versions of this exercise by thinking of anything or anyone you love, establishing the feeling, then sending it forth into our world. Keep doing this! Our world needs us all to focus right now on the wonderful commonalities we all share so we can continue to create the peaceful world we all envision.

Summing Up

You can learn a lot about yourself and your soul's journey by delving into your past life connections with animals. The animals that show up during various times in our history make a meaningful impact on our experience by enriching our lives.

Remember to take notes, and also remember you can always try these journeys again if you want to find out about more past lives. Personally, I use regression as a tool and I know at any given moment, whatever comes up is exactly what's meant to be. New information may be revealed later.

CONCLUSION

OH, HOW TIME FLIES. My little love BisKit is now already ten years old. It's hard to believe so many years have passed since I delivered him from the animal shelter so long ago. I know a painful goodbye is looming, and yet the old saying "it's better to have loved and lost than never to have loved at all" is so very, very true. I wouldn't trade a single moment with BisKit, Goo, Scruffster, or any of my beloved animals. I'm sure you feel the same about your pets.

How could we possibly live full lives without the love of our pets? Animals bring us unconditional love and the chance for giving, sharing, and learning about ourselves and others through their eyes. Life is exponentially richer as a result of our dogs, cats, birds, and the like, but in order to receive those learnings and benefits, we must jump in with both feet and with eyes wide open to realize that, unfortunately, nothing in the Universe lasts. This planet we signed up for has some good things going for it, but one of the most difficult aspects of life is the fact that nobody will get out alive, and at every given second, things change and dissolve.

Pets feel grief as deeply as we do, which is another connection we all share. The difference is they don't have the capacity to intellectualize their loss, which can be either good or bad, depending on how you look at it. We humans tend to dwell on our grief at times, which is more than understandable, but at some point, we can hopefully move past our loss to a place of greater peace and acceptance. Past life regression has been a godsend for me and my clients, particularly for helping resolve grief and accepting the universal condition of impermanence so we can keep on loving and embrace the wisdom of change and the unknown.

Exploring the past incarnations we've shared with our animals isn't a mere amusement. Of course, we discover entertaining stories and memories of the good times and loving exchanges we share, but often the animals help us uncover and heal raw emotions and traumas. They understand our unconscious motivations and behaviors better than our human counterparts. When we love an animal, we put our whole body, mind, and soul into that relationship and our pet becomes the projection of all the unconscious sentiments we present to them. By so doing, our pets give us the greatest gift any living soul can—the opportunity to heal and become better souls. No doubt for those who believe in a progression of evolution that we experience by reincarnating through several life-forms, owning and loving animals puts a star on our universal report card and helps us improve our karma, evolving all our relationships with others, the environment, and the world at large in an effort to improve the human condition.

My hope is that this book gives you cause to smile at the blessing animals are in your life, and I hope knowing we will see our pets in the afterlife and in our future lives may help you heal when those losses do occur, so you can look back on your pet relationships with love and fond memories and know you were blessed to have them while they were in your life. That's how I choose to view my animal relationships. No matter the duration, I am better for them, and for as long as I live in my current life, I will embrace the temporal aspects of life and love my pets for as long as they'll have me. With that, I send you love and light on your journey and wish you and your pets all the joy this world has to offer. Namaste!

BIBLIOGRAPHY

Alderton, David. *The Complete Illustrated Encyclopedia of Birds of the World: The Ultimate Reference Source and Identifier for 1,600 Birds, Profiling Habitat, Plumage, Nesting and Food.* Leicestershire, England: Lorenz Books, 2012.

———. *Foxes, Wolves and Wild Dogs of the World.* New York: Facts on File, Inc., 1994.

Anastasi, Donna. *Gerbils: The Complete Guide to Gerbil Care.* Irvine, CA: BowTie Press, 2005.

Andrews, Ted. *Animal Speak: The Spiritual & Magical Powers of Creatures Great & Small.* St. Paul, MN: Llewellyn Publications, 1993.

Bartlett, Patricia. *The Hamster Handbook.* Hauppauge, NY: Barron's Educational Series, Inc., 2015.

Bernstein, Morey. *The Search for Bridey Murphy.* New York: Doubleday, 1989.

Busch, Robert H. *The Wolf Almanac, New and Revised: A Celebration of Wolves and Their World.* Landham, MD: Lyons Press, 2007.

Cameron, W. Bruce. *A Dog's Journey: Another Novel for Humans.* New York: A Forge Book, 2012.

————. *A Dog's Way Home: A Novel.* New York: A Forge book, 2017.

Cheek, Roland. *Learning to Talk Bear: So Bears Can Listen.* Columbia Falls, MT: Skyline Publishing, 1997.

Daly, Carol Himsel, D.V.M., and Sharon Vanderlip, D.V.M. *Rats: Everything About Purchase, Care, Nutrition, Handling and Behavior.* Hauppauge, NY: Barron's Educational Series, Inc., 2012.

Grogan, John. *Marley & Me: Life and Love with the World's Worst Dog.* New York: Harper Collins, 2005.

Holloway, April. "Dealing in the Past: How Did Ancient Egyptians Get Nicotine and Cocaine?" 2 December 2017, https://www .ancient-origins.net/history/dealing-past-how-did-ancient-egyp tians-get-nicotine-and-cocaine-009223.

Koontz, Dean. *A Big Little Life: A Memoir of a Joyful Dog.* New York: Harper Collins, 2009.

Mattison, Chris. *Smithsonian Nature Guide: Snakes and Other Reptiles and Amphibians: The World in Your Hands.* New York: DK Publishing, 2014.

Mills, Dick. *Eyewitness Handbooks Aquarium Fish: The Visual Guide to More than 500 Marine and Freshwater Fish Varieties.* New York: Dorling Kindersley, Inc., 1993.

Orban, Timothy. *German Shepherd—Popular Dog Library.* Neptune City, NJ: T.F.H. Publications, Inc., 1999.

Pavia, Audrey. *Guinea Pig: Your Happy Healthy Pet, Second Edition.* Hoboken, NJ: Howell Book House, 2005.

Seidensticker, John, and Susan Lumpkin. *Cats: Smithsonian Answer Book.* Washington, D.C.: Smithsonian Books, 2004.

Skomal, Gregory. *The Shark Handbook: Second Edition: The Definitive Guide to the World's Most Fascinating Sharks.* Kennebunkport, ME: Cider Mill Press, 2008.

Stebbins, Robert C. *Peterson Field Guides Western Reptiles and Amphibians Third Edition.* New York: Houghton Mifflin Company, 2003.

Stone, Lynn M. *Rabbit Breeds: The Pocket Guide to 49 Essential Breeds.* North Adams, MA: Storey Publishing, 2016.

ANIMAL RESOURCES

WITH FEW EXCEPTIONS, MOST of my pets were adopted through local city animal shelter and animal rescue organizations. Whether you have a pet now or you're looking to find one, here's a list of resources you can use to find animals to adopt. If you want to find meaningful volunteer work in your community or donate to the worthy cause of helping animals who give so much to us through their loving presence, here are a few good places to start:

Adopt a Greyhound: http://www.adopt-a-greyhound.org/

Animal Rescue League of North Texas: You may have a rescue league in your state. Check the internet for further information: http://www.arltexas.org/

Animal Services: Find contact details for your town and connect with your local animal shelter.

Humane Society: https://www.humanesociety.org/

Petfinder.com: Connects you with adoptable pets in your area. My city uses this site to help connect residents with animals: https://www.petfinder.com/

The Shelter Pet Project: https://theshelterpetproject.org/

The following is a list of some top organizations dedicated to the care of animals:

American Society for the Prevention of Cruelty to Animals: https://secure.aspca.org/

People for the Ethical Treatment of Animals (PETA): https://www.peta.org/

World Wildlife Fund: helps endangered species https://www.worldwildlife.org/

To Write to the Author

If you wish to contact the author or would like more information about this book, please write to the author in care of Llewellyn Worldwide Ltd. and we will forward your request. Both the author and the publisher appreciate hearing from you and learning of your enjoyment of this book and how it has helped you. Llewellyn Worldwide Ltd. cannot guarantee that every letter written to the author can be answered, but all will be forwarded. Please write to:

Shelley A. Kaehr, PhD
℅ Llewellyn Worldwide
2143 Wooddale Drive
Woodbury, MN 55125-2989

Please enclose a self-addressed stamped envelope for reply,
or $1.00 to cover costs. If outside the U.S.A., enclose
an international postal reply coupon.

Many of Llewellyn's authors have websites with additional information and resources. For more information, please visit our website at http://www.llewellyn.com.